MW01253372

The Methamphetamine Industry in America

CRITICAL ISSUES IN CRIME AND SOCIETY

Raymond J. Michalowski, Series Editor

Critical Issues in Crime and Society is oriented toward critical analysis of contemporary problems in crime and justice. The series is open to a broad range of topics including specific types of crime, wrongful behavior by economically or politically powerful actors, controversies over justice system practices, and issues related to the intersection of identity, crime, and justice. It is committed to offering thoughtful works that will be accessible to scholars and professional criminologists, general readers, and students.

For a list of titles in the series, see the last page of the book.

The Methamphetamine Industry in America

Transnational Cartels and Local Entrepreneurs

Henry H. Brownstein,
Timothy M. Mulcahy,
and Johannes Huessy

Rutgers University Press
New Brunswick, New Jersey, and London

LIBRARY OF CONGRESS CATALOGING–IN–PUBLICATION DATA

Brownstein, Henry H.
    The methamphetamine industry in America / Henry H. Brownstein, Timothy
M. Mulcahy, Johannes Huessy
        pages cm.—(Critical issues in crime and society)
    Includes bibliographical references and index.
    ISBN 978-0-8135-6984-0 (hardcover : alk. paper)—ISBN 978-0-8135-6986-4
(e-book)
    1. Methamphetamine abuse—United States. 2. Drug abuse--Social aspects—
United States. 3. Drug control—United States. 4. Drug control—Mexico. I.
Mulcahy, Timothy M., 1968–II. Huessy, Johannes, 1982–III. Title.

    HV5822.M38B76 2014
    363.450973—dc23
    2013040664

    A British Cataloging-in-Publication record for this book is available
                from the British Library.

    Visit our website: http://rutgerspress.rutgers.edu

    Manufactured in the United States of America

Henry H. Brownstein
To my wife Cindy, for being there and understanding me

Timothy M. Mulcahy
To my daughter Reilly and son Brendan,
"stay true to the dreams of thy youth"

Johannes Huessy
For the reckless ones whose bad trip left them cold

CONTENTS

Preface   vii
Acknowledgments   ix

1   *Understanding Methamphetamine Markets as an Industry*   1

2   *Methamphetamine in America*   13

3   *Social Activity in the Methamphetamine Industry*   29

4   *Social Relationships in the Methamphetamine Industry*   55

5   *The Culture of the Methamphetamine Industry*   77

6   *Meth Markets and the Methamphetamine Industry in the United States*   97

Appendix: The Study of the Dynamics of Methamphetamine Markets   111
References   127
Index   137

PREFACE

THIS BOOK TELLS THE STORY of how the illicit methamphetamine industry in America survived and even thrived despite efforts to control it by legislation and law enforcement. It is based on a study of methamphetamine markets all across the United States and tells the story of those markets from the perspective and in the words of people whose lives have been personally linked to these markets in one way or another. In addition it draws on our years of combined experience studying illicit drugs, drug users, and drug markets.

For four years from 2007 to 2011 we studied methamphetamine markets with funding from the National Institute on Drug Abuse (NIDA, R21DA024391). Our study was part of a research initiative supported by NIDA and the National Institute of Justice (NIJ). We conducted a mixed methods, three-stage study starting with an exploratory screening survey of 1,367 police agencies across the country, followed by open-ended and in-depth telephone interviews with fifty narcotics police in departments around the country, and finally site visits for observations and personal interviews in and around almost thirty cities and towns in five regions of the country. We concluded that the methamphetamine industry in America is strong and adaptable and in the twenty-first century is not only surviving but thriving. This does not diminish our observation while visiting communities with active methamphetamine markets that while business is good its impact on public health and public safety is not. Notably, we found that while federal and state legislation designed to address meth-related problems initially did inconvenience the markets and marketers of meth, it also had unintended outcomes including the revitalization and reorganization of what was previously a more localized yet fragmented industry.

This book provides a broad perspective through which we present the story of what we learned about methamphetamine as an industry. However, our story is not told from the perspective of industrial economics, describing business techniques used to produce or market products or the details of practices designed to maximize revenue and profits. Nor is it told from the public health perspective, describing how the use of methamphetamine affects the health and well-being of the people who use it and the people around them. And it is not told from the perspective of law enforcement, concerned with how to control the use of an illegal substance and other crimes that might or might not be the work of people who use or deal in that substance. Rather this book looks at methamphetamine markets and the methamphetamine industry from a sociological perspective, viewing them through the eyes and words of the people who participate in them and explores the ways they live their lives among other people in the shadow of methamphetamine use and transactions.

As a sociological analysis of methamphetamine markets and the methamphetamine industry in America, this book views the markets and the industry as social organizations comprised of people. The focus is on those people and how their actions and behavior form social patterns as they interact with each other and relate to one another in a culturally defined context. This is not to diminish the importance of understanding and explaining methamphetamine markets or the methamphetamine industry in economic terms or the impact of the drug and its use and production and distribution on people or communities. It is just another way to look at things that sheds new light on our understanding of and appreciation for the significance and impacts of the markets and the industry, a way that has not received much attention before. In this book we demonstrate the importance of understanding methamphetamine, and by extension other drugs, in society at the broadest level through a sociological lens that focuses on the structure of social activity and behavior, social interaction and social relationships, and cultural elements that shape the organization and operation of a nationwide methamphetamine industry and its realization through regional and local markets. The focus is on the experiences of people as members of society and communities who participate in or are affected by their own actions and behavior and that of others around them who participate in the world of methamphetamine.

Acknowledgments

As NOTED EARLIER, this book is based on four years of research conducted from 2007 through 2011. The work was a study called the Dynamics of Methamphetamine Markets and was funded in part by a grant from the National Institute on Drug Abuse. Additional support was made available by our employer, NORC at the University of Chicago. Funding from the NORC Center for Excellence in Survey Research (CESR) provided partial support for the preparation of this manuscript. The funding from NIDA was part of a collaborative effort between NIDA and the National Institute of Justice (NIJ) called the Joint Initiative for Research on Retail Drug Markets.

Without the support of NIDA and without the efforts and determination of Yonette Thomas, who was then the Branch Chief of the Epidemiology Research Branch in the Division of Epidemiology, Services and Prevention Research at NIDA, it would not have been possible to conduct this research. We are grateful to Yonette, who left NIDA to become the Associate Vice President for Research Compliance at Howard University in Washington, DC. Bethany Deeds subsequently took over as our NIDA Project Officer and played a major role not only in helping keep the project moving forward but also in helping to keep our work focused and on track. At NORC we thank Dan Gaylin, Eric Goplerud, Chet Bowie, and especially Dan Kasprzyk, who heads CESR, for their encouragement and support.

During the period of the research we wrote several papers and gave several presentations. In addition to the papers presented at professional association meetings, we also presented findings and ideas to meetings of the Joint NIDA-NIJ Initiative and to various federal government agencies. We thank Linda Truitt at NIJ, who organized the NIDA-NIJ

Initiative meetings. We also thank Michael Cala and Terry Zobeck at the Office of National Drug Control Policy (ONDCP), Gam Rose at the U.S. Drug Enforcement Administration (DEA), and David Levin, formerly at DEA.

We three were involved in doing this research including planning and writing the proposal, fielding the survey, conducting interviews, visiting sites, and analyzing data and writing reports and papers from the beginning to the end and beyond. However, a number of other colleagues and associates worked with us at various points and they all made critical contributions to the research. We want to thank Carol Hafford, Susan Martin, Dan Woods, Bruce Kubu, and Kathleen Parks. In particular we want to thank Phyllis Newton, who worked with us at NORC when we were designing the study and writing the proposal. We also give special thanks to Bruce Taylor, who contributed a great deal at the early stages when we were designing the study when he was Research Director at the Police Executive Research Forum (PERF) and later (when he joined us at NORC) to analyzing survey data, joining us on a few site visits, and writing papers and articles. Also, while we were in the Midwest visiting sites Ralph Weisheit, a professor at Illinois State University who studies methamphetamine users and markets, joined us at a few sites and we thank him for his contribution.

During the first year of the research we held a meeting of an Advisory Panel to help guide our study. They gave us a number of good ideas, including the suggestion to collect more data from the survey than we had originally planned. We thank the members of that panel including Bruce Bellamy (Division Commander, Metro Patrol Division, Charlotte-Mecklenburg Police Department), Cindy Burke (San Diego Regional Planning Agency, Criminal Justice Research Division), Kelly Damphousse (University of Oklahoma), Rick Harwood (then at the Lewin Group), Denise Herz (California State University at Los Angeles), Toni Krupski (University of Washington), Jane Maxwell (University of Texas), Tom Mieczkowski (University of South Florida), Kevin O'Sullivan (Commander, St. Louis Police Department), and Diane Wiscarson (Diane Frost Wiscarson, PC).

We thank Ray Michalowski, an Arizona Regents' Professor at Northern Arizona University and Series Editor of the series of which this book is part, Critical Issues in Crime and Society. We also thank, again, Tom Mieczkowski, a professor at the University of South Florida. They both read an early draft of this book and gave us very useful comments that helped make the book better. And we give special thanks to Peter Mickulas, our editor at Rutgers University Press. From the very beginning he saw the value in what we had done and what we wanted to do. As we wrote he provided us with guidance and support through which the book progressed from a long academic essay to a thought-provoking and compelling narrative that tells the fascinating story of how the methamphetamine industry in America evolved at the start of the twenty-first century. This would be a different and less interesting book without his guidance. We also thank John Raymond for copyediting what we thought was the final version of our book and making it more readable. And we thank Carrie Hudak for helping us turn a manuscript into a book.

We thank Jesse Hambrick Jr., sergeant in charge of the Drug and Gang Prevention Unit of the Douglas County Sheriff's Department in Georgia, for the cover photo, but more than that we are grateful to him for introducing us to so many people involved with methamphetamine and for teaching us so much about the methamphetamine business. In the end, our greatest thanks go to all the people all over America who shared their time and stories with us. That includes all of the 1,367 people who responded to our survey, the fifty people who told us the story of methamphetamine in their jurisdiction and shared an Internet connection with us during our telephone interviews, and the hundreds of people who spoke to us in and around almost thirty cities, towns, and rural communities in five regions of the country. As much as we would like to we cannot name them. But while we respect the confidentiality of their identities we cannot thank them enough for their contribution to this work. It is an understatement to say that without them this book would not be possible.

While we thank everyone for their help and support, we take full responsibility for what we wrote. Opinions and points of view herein are ours alone and do not necessarily reflect those of any other individual or organization, including NORC, NIDA, and NIJ or any of the many gracious regional, state, and local law enforcement, public health, family service, drug treatment, and other community agencies and people that participated in our study.

*The Methamphetamine
Industry in America*

CHAPTER I

Understanding Methamphetamine Markets as an Industry

GALAX IS LOCATED IN VIRGINIA just north of the border with North Carolina and just south of the Great Appalachian Valley. It sits about twenty-five hundred feet above sea level at the gateway to the Blue Ridge Mountains. Summers are mild and humid and winters can be cold and snowy. Every August the people of Galax celebrate "the largest Old Time Bluegrass Fiddler's Convention" and that, along with many other music and craft festivals and conventions, makes the city "the World Capital of Old Time Mountain Music." People from all over the world visit Galax and the surrounding area to enjoy the music and dance, to compete for prizes, to explore the scenic countryside, and to wander through the quaint downtown shops.

Galax was incorporated as a town in 1906 just after the Norfolk and Western Railway extended a spur to the area, and then separated itself from surrounding Grayson and Carroll Counties during the 1950s. According to a centennial history written by Brian Funk, the editor of the *Gazette* in Galax, with the arrival of the railroad Galax emerged as a center for the manufacturing of furniture, textiles, and hardwood flooring. For decades the furniture industry thrived in the area until the national, regional, and local economy began to decline and eventually only one furniture factory remained. With the closing of the factories came the loss of jobs and growing rates of unemployment. A place cannot survive as a viable community in the absence of work that people can do to earn a living, so as one industry moves away another needs to take its place. Galax has managed to endure and arguably prosper by embracing its musical and artistic heritage and building a thriving tourist industry.

According to the 2010 Census the population of Galax is 7,042 people, an increase of 3 percent since the last census in 2000 (City of Galax,

Virginia 2013). The median household income in 2009 in Galax was $21,744, compared to $59,330 in Virginia, and the median home value in the city was $84,132 compared to $252,600 in the state. Among those who are counted in the census, the proportion of people living in Galax who are foreign born is slightly higher than the statewide proportion (8.6 percent compared to 8.1 percent), with most of those reportedly coming from Latin America. The proportion of the local population that is Hispanic exceeds the proportion in the rest of the state. In 2012 unemployment in the city was 8.1 percent compared to 5.7 percent statewide.

During a visit to Galax and the surrounding area in the summer of 2011 we found good people who were hard working and cared about taking care of themselves, their families, and their community. The problem is that while tourism does create jobs and produce income it is not the only lucrative activity to have taken root in the area. In the early twenty-first century in rural, southern Virginia, as global manufacturing industry has fled not only tourism but the international methamphetamine industry has also found fertile ground.

In response to a survey we sent in 2009 to police agencies across the country, we learned from the police in Galax that like many other places around the country a disproportionate number of the drug arrests they were making involved methamphetamine. They reported only small amounts of methamphetamine being produced in what could be called local laboratories, while most of it was being imported from Mexico. And as we found true in most places around the country, typically the methamphetamine being used by local people was being sold not in public, but in private places, particularly homes. Our police survey respondents in Galax told us that methamphetamine was a "very serious problem" for them. So when we chose agencies from among those that had responded to our survey to call and conduct a personal interview, we included Galax.

During our telephone interview with the police in Galax they again told us that most of their drug arrests involved methamphetamine, and most of the methamphetamine came from Mexico. We asked whether the trade in methamphetamine was different from the trade in other drugs, like heroin or cocaine. The police respondent replied that with methamphetamine, "the dealers, the wholesale distributors, tend to be Hispanic. We're starting to see large amounts of money. We're seeing some wholesale points. We may [arrest] a Mexican that's in a mobile home with a mattress, a television, VCR, and refrigerator. And all he does is to distribute quantities of methamphetamine, collect money, and give [the money] to somebody who comes to pick it up." When we started our research in 2007 we expected to find people cooking methamphetamine in their homes and selling what they cooked to people in their community. We did not expect to find dealers devoid of local ties. So we decided to include Galax as a place we would visit during the third stage of our study, the site visits.

Galax was one of the first places we visited for our study of the dynamics of methamphetamine markets. And what we learned there changed everything for us. We started out thinking of methamphetamine markets primarily as local mom-and-pop businesses operated on a small scale by individual cooks who made small amounts of product to serve a small number of local users. We knew that the federal and state legislation from the middle of the first decade of the twenty-first century, which was intended to limit access to the necessary ingredients to make methamphetamine, such as the pseudoephedrine found in ordinary cold tablets, had made it more difficult for local cooks to stay in business. We had heard and read that the importation of methamphetamine from Mexico was on the rise. What we did not realize was how far the product being imported from Mexico had spread and how complex the business around it had become. What we saw in Galax was not a community of meth-involved people making and using methamphetamine simply to get high or even to blur any pain in their lives resulting from the loss of local businesses and jobs. What we saw first in Galax and then later across the United States was an example of how methamphetamine had become a major industry in cities, towns, and rural communities across America, creating jobs for people who needed work and serving for some people as a focus for their daily lives and social experience.

We spoke to many people in the Galax area, including not only the police who had participated in our survey and interviews but also drug treatment counselors, social service providers, government officials, methamphetamine users, and meth dealers. Our interviews were open ended to allow us to fill in the details of what we had learned earlier. We asked a local police officer who worked narcotics cases how methamphetamine moves into the Galax area. The officer told us what they had discovered over the past several years through working with federal agency partners on a case involving methamphetamine. The methamphetamine, we were told, is coming to Galax from Mexico

> across the border in Texas straight up to Chicago, from there straight up to Tennessee, and then [from] Tennessee to Galax. That was pretty much the route. Some of the players we had worked were told to "drive this truck to [a corner in Chicago] to a Food Lion, and park this truck at the Food Lion and call this number when you get there. There'll be a red pickup or a gold Lexus or whatever. Get in that vehicle. Leave. We'll call you back, maybe that day, maybe the next morning." They call back and say okay go back and get your truck at [a particular location]. You get in your truck and drive it back to Tennessee or Galax. [The driver] doesn't know if he brought money out or brought dope back.

More recently the Galax police are finding that methamphetamine has been coming to Galax through Atlanta, which they described as "the hotbed" for transporting the drug along the Eastern Seaboard. Galax itself is a hub in this transportation route. After it arrives in Galax methamphetamine gets distributed to surrounding towns, like "Staunton and the Waynesboro area."

We learned in Galax that the production of methamphetamine and its distribution to towns and cities in the United States was not simply a matter of local people cooking meth for their neighbors. Galax was a hub for the regional distribution of methamphetamine, part of a national network through which high-quality methamphetamine produced in Mexico was being distributed to users. And on the local level the distribution to users from the local sellers was no less well organized. One person in Galax told us how he got into the business of selling methamphetamine after starting to use the drug while he still had a legitimate job and was making a reasonable living doing construction work. As his addiction took hold he spent more time and money on the drug and worked less at his job. He started to think about how he could live being high all the time without having to work. Through a woman he knew he was introduced to a Mexican man she knew who offered him an opportunity. The first time the man received some meth on consignment from his new acquaintance from Mexico he was told that he could pay for it after he sold it. So he got started taking small amounts to be able to sell enough to support his habit. Eventually, he told us, "Mexicans showed up at my house. And once you start in with the Mexicans, they're in competition with each other." He explained that over time different individual distributors who had recently moved to the area from Mexico and who were responsible for establishing the local market on behalf of the Mexican business organizations or cartels offered him deals to work for them to sell their product to local consumers. He needed the wholesale distributors working for the Mexican manufacturers to supply the product for his local business (and his habit), and they needed him to reach the local consumer population who would only buy from people they knew and trusted. It was "strictly business," as he described it.

The main lesson we first learned in Galax is that methamphetamine is a thriving industry in the United States. That does not necessarily mean there are users everywhere or even that there are large numbers of users in any particular place, including Galax. What it does mean is that local methamphetamine markets are organized and operate as integral cogs in a national, indeed an international, industry. In this book we write about what we learned from our study of methamphetamine markets in cities, towns, rural communities, and neighborhoods all across the United States. We describe and explain how methamphetamine markets are organized and operate as part of this larger industry, and how at the local level methamphetamine users and the people who sell to them are part of a community of people whose social lives are interwoven through their common interest in buying and selling methamphetamine and getting high.

RESEARCH ON ILLICIT DRUG MARKETS

Obviously we are not the first team of researchers ever to study illicit drug markets, nor even the first to study methamphetamine markets. What distinguishes our study is the way we combined a broad overview of what was happening on the national level with the details of how the markets are organized and operate in different parts of the country and in different communities. Our focus from the beginning has been sociological rather than economic. We did not start by asking direct questions about supply and demand or price and purity of the product. We set out to understand how people who participate in methamphetamine markets organize and operate those markets and how the organization and operation of those markets connects them to other each other and to other people. Our plan was to study the institutional arrangements they fashioned to make the markets work, as well as the social relationships among the participants themselves and with other people around them, including people like family, friends, and neighbors. We wanted to understand how being a participant in a methamphetamine market shaped the daily life of market participants as members of a community, and how it gave meaning to their social experience and personal relationships.

To know where to begin we had to know what to look for. We needed to be able to define what we meant by an illicit drug market. In 1863 President Abraham Lincoln signed an Act creating the National Academy of Sciences (NAS) to provide independent and authoritative advice to the government on matters related to science, engineering, and medicine (National Academy of Sciences 2013a). As a component of the Academy, the National Research Council through its Divisions and Committees holds meetings and produces expert reports to disseminate knowledge in order to inform public policy and action in areas related to the public good (National Academy of Sciences 2013b). In a 2001 report on illegal drugs and drug policy in the United States, the National Research Council defined an illicit retail drug market as the set of people, facilities, and procedures through which illicit drugs are transferred from sellers or dealers to buyers or users. In that sense a retail illicit drug business is the sum of commercial relationships and transactions that facilitate the proximate transfer of illicit substances for personal use. But for a retail drug market to operate in a particular place there must also be means and methods for the production and wholesale distribution of whatever illicit substance or substances are to be exchanged in the local marketplace. And there must be a reason and way for the market to take root and prosper in a community of people.

So while there has been a fair amount of research already done on illicit drug markets, for the most part it does not address the interrelatedness of local markets with the national and international drug industry, and it almost always views the markets as economic enterprises and rarely as social phenomena. Much of the research on the traffic and trade in illicit drugs in the United States has been about regional and local markets. Further, while a variety of research methods and approaches have been used to study illicit drug markets in the United States that research has been largely about New York or Chicago. For example, in the 1960s and early 1970s when heroin was the illicit drug that drew the greatest amount of public and media attention and concern, Patrick Hughes and his colleagues conducted a pioneering epidemiological study of heroin users and markets in Chicago that for the first time identified a differentiated system of roles among users and dealers. During the 1980s when powder cocaine replaced heroin as the drug of primary concern, Terry Williams wrote about the lives of eight teenagers he studied in the Bronx and the Washington Heights and Harlem sections of Manhattan who found work in the local cocaine business given the absence of legitimate employment opportunities. Later also in New York from the late 1980s into the 1990s, when crack replaced powder cocaine as the drug of choice and concern, Philippe Bourgois conducted an ethnographic study in Spanish Harlem and exposed the truth that people involved in the crack trade may work in an underground economy but like all other people they spend their lives struggling for subsistence and dignity.

Criminologists have also conducted studies of illicit retail drug markets, since anything outside of the law is fair game for the study of crime. Given attention to the illegal nature of the drug trade many criminologists have studied drug markets in the context of law enforcement strategy and practice and have explicitly focused on particular drugs in particular locations. For example, during the 1990s, based on findings of a study of the geography of drug dealing in San Diego, John Eck concluded that he could explain strategies used by retail drug sellers and buyers (i.e., transacting only with people they know versus dealing with anyone, including strangers) in relation to the risk of being caught in a web of law enforcement. In 2000, in a study of drug hot spots in Newark, New Jersey, David Weisburd and Lorraine Mazerolle found that areas where drug transactions take place account for more arrests and calls for police service even when the crimes involved are not specifically related to drugs.

Other criminologists have studied illicit drug markets in terms of the relationship between drug market activity and other criminal or deviant activity, such as violence or gang participation. In 1985 Paul Goldstein suggested that one of the ways drugs and violence can be related, what he called systemic violence, involves people doing violent things as a result of their participation in the normally aggressive patterns of interaction within systems of drug use and distribution. During the 1980s and

1990s, in New York, Goldstein, Henry Brownstein, and their colleagues conducted a number of studies showing how dealers fighting over territory or buyers angry about the quality of drugs they purchased resulted in violent assault, sometimes going as far as homicide. Regarding the relationship between drug market activity and gangs, through interviews with inmates in California prisons during the late 1980s Jerome Skolnick and his associates found that the level of involvement of gangs with drugs and drug markets varied in different parts of the state.

Like the ethnographic and criminological studies of illicit drug markets, studies of the economy of drug markets likewise have focused on particular markets in particular places. In 1990 Peter Reuter and his colleagues estimated the number of people involved in the illicit retail street drug trade and calculated the earnings of individuals who were charged with a criminal offense and included in a Pretrial Services database in Washington, DC, between 1985 and 1987. More recently, in a study of illegal drug markets, Travis Taniguchi and his colleagues found that in Philadelphia drug dealers are spatially clustered.

Research about the illicit drug trade on the national or international levels has similarly been about drug trafficking as a criminal enterprise or about the economy of the trade. Using available data from crime statistics and reports by the Office of National Drug Control Policy (ONDCP), in a recent analysis Jonathan Caulkins and Peter Reuter studied the stability of prices in the illicit drug trade on a national level and concluded that the legal prohibition of drugs with more than a base level of enforcement drives up the price of drugs beyond what the price would be in a legal market. Frederick Desroches reviewed the research on upper-level drug trafficking in the United States, the United Kingdom, Canada, and the Netherlands and concluded that drug trafficking is a hierarchical system involving importation, manufacturing, cultivation, distribution, and sale of illicit drugs and that we still have a lot to learn about how it all works and fits together.

Specifically, for methamphetamine, a few studies have focused on local retail markets without reference to the larger context of national or international connections. In the early 2000s Henry Brownstein and Bruce Taylor used data from surveys of arrestees in ten cities around the United States and found that local methamphetamine markets in different cities vary in their stability. During the last decade Rebecca McKetin and her associates conducted a study of the methamphetamine market in Sydney, Australia, and concluded that the local market had changed since the 1990s with increasing levels of product purity because the market was being supplied not only by local production but also by imported crystalline meth.

From our study of local markets in regions across America we repeatedly heard the same assertion about local methamphetamine markets from the police we surveyed or interviewed and from the people we spoke with during our visits to their communities. If we were going to understand the local retail methamphetamine markets we needed to view them from the broader perspective of their place in the national methamphetamine industry and even its ties to the methamphetamine industry based in Mexico. And we would need to appreciate the markets and the industry not only as an economic organization but as a social organization as well.

DRUG MARKETS AND INDUSTRY AS SOCIAL ORGANIZATIONS

Overall, the findings of the extant body of research on illicit drug markets inform our understanding of local retail drug markets in particular locations and cumulatively across the country. What they do not do is give us a broad and comprehensive view of the interrelatedness of local retail markets for illicit drugs, even for the same illicit drug, across local and regional boundaries and crossing from retail to wholesale manufacture and distribution. The ethnographic studies provide great detail and depth, but only for a very small number of people on a very limited location for a narrow area of social activity. The criminological studies may cover a larger number of people and a wider area of activity, but they are limited to a narrow focus on illicit drug markets as a form or source of illegitimate behavior or activity. Economic studies may have a national or regional as well as a local focus, but they limit their attention to markets as commercial ventures.

Another way to think about an illicit drug market is to conceptualize it as a social organization. Talcott Parsons, the prominent sociological theorist of the mid-twentieth century, defined a social organization as a collectivity of people who organize themselves to work together primarily to attain a common specified goal. That goal in turn is defined in relation to the relevant aspects of the larger social environment or context of which it is a part and has some impact on that environment or context. Illicit retail drug markets are collectivities with the specific goal of transferring a particular substance or substances from sellers to buyers when that substance is deemed to have no lawful purpose in the surrounding community. So perhaps the greater significance of the extant research on illicit retail drug markets is what it tells us about the extent to which the organization and operation of illicit drug markets can vary even in a single place, and about the different ways that market participants relate to each other in different markets and different places. That is, the research on illicit retail drug markets in the United States demonstrates the wide range of social organization, social activity, and social relationships that comprise the business of selling and buying illicit drugs for personal use in America and why it is important to understand the broader environment or context of which that business is part.

The Office of National Drug Control Policy is a component of the Executive Office of the President created by the Anti-Drug Abuse Act of 1988 to advise the president on drug control issues, coordinate drug control activities and funding for the government, and to produce an annual National Control Strategy (Office of National Drug Control Policy 2013). The National Drug Intelligence Center (NDIC) was established in 1993 by the Department of Defense Appropriations Act and closed in 2012 when its responsibility was shifted to the Drug Enforcement Agency of the Department of Justice (National Drug Intelligence Center 2013). While active it was responsible for the coordination and consolidation of drug intelligence from a variety of sources. Although most research and consequently most of what we know about illicit drug markets comes from studies of retail markets in particular locations, federal agencies such as ONDCP and the NDIC have recognized the wide-ranging national and international scale and scope of drug markets operating in the United States. So too have analysts of drug policy in general. Consequently, although problems related to illegal drugs are often considered local problems, the work of drug policy analysts supports the conclusion that illicit drug markets are better understood and addressed in a more comprehensive context. Although we can learn about and respond to specific localized drug problems by studying and concentrating on local retail markets, by viewing those markets in the broader context of the drug industry we can see how the problems as well as the social activity of those markets in different areas are interrelated and why that matters.

Even for industrial economists the distinction between industry and markets has not always been clear and it is not uncommon for them to have been treated as synonymous. But while they are related they are also different and that difference is important. In his early but influential writing on the subject, in 1949 P. W. S. Andrews defined "industry" as groupings of individual *businesses* sharing common techniques and processes to produce a specified commodity and "market" as the grouping of *consumers* for the product of an industry. While these definitions may have evolved over time, the point for our purpose is that industry and market do not refer to the same thing but *together* they define the universe of social activity and relationships from production through distribution to consumption of a commodity, in this case methamphetamine.

Among economic sociologists who study the sociology of markets there has been concern in recent years about internal disagreements among social scientists who explain markets. Nonetheless there is some level of agreement that the study of markets from a sociological perspective requires different approaches for explaining them. Specifically, it requires an approach that distinctly and distinctively emphasizes social activity and institutions, social networks and relationships, and the substance of the social experience of the markets including things such as practices, meanings, ideas, technology, and standards or what is commonly called culture. Emphasizing points of agreement, Neil Fligstein and Luke Dauter have argued that sociologists of markets need not look past each other but rather should look at their differences in terminology and perspective to best be able to make sense of empirical cases. In that spirit, for this book we studied individual methamphetamine markets in locations around the country to understand how they are organized and operate on the local level and how they are related across the country through their shared experience as part of the same industry. In doing so we considered social patterns and institutions through which markets are organized and operate, social relationships among market participants and between market participants and the people around them, and cultural experience and factors related to each market studied and to the relationships between and among markets. In summary, this book is a sociological study of the illicit methamphetamine industry and markets in the United States based on the belief that illicit drug markets are social organizations.

In this book we tell the story of how methamphetamine markets evolved in the United States over more than a decade given changes in public policies and practices and changing public opinion about methamphetamine as a drug. In the later chapters of this book we tell that story looking closely at the markets as part of a larger industry and how they are socially organized and how they operate, the relationships among the people involved with the markets and the people around them, and the national, regional, and local culture of the markets. Our story is based on our own national research over four years with emphasis on the five regions of the country we visited. It builds on the research that has already been done and what is already known about methamphetamine and meth markets. To provide background for our story, in the next chapter we describe how and why we conducted our research the way we did and say something about methamphetamine as a drug and about the contemporary state of knowledge and history of methamphetamine and its markets in the United States.

CHAPTER 2

Methamphetamine in America

WITH ITS WORLD-CLASS AIRPORT and its placement at the intersection of both east-west and north-south interstate highways, the region around Atlanta, Georgia, is in an excellent spot through which to transport products from around the nation and even the world to consumers in other parts of the country. One online business magazine, *Inc.*, describes the Atlanta area as follows, in a March 1, 2004, article by Joel Kotkin, "Top 25 Cities for Doing Business in America": "Spread out over 28 counties in north-central Georgia, Atlanta's region includes over 4.5 million people, only 420,000 of whom live in the city itself. It combines the advantages seen in smaller communities with an array of assets—such as top-flight universities, major corporate headquarters, and a world-class airport—usually only found in leading global cities" (Kotkin 2004). So it is not surprising that during the early years of the twenty-first century the area around Atlanta, Georgia, became a hub for the distribution of methamphetamine from Mexico to towns and cities throughout the eastern states of the United States. The shipments carrying the drugs travel mostly in trucks heading east from Texas along interstate highways into and through Atlanta where I-20 going west to east intersects with both I-75 and I-85 going south to north. Then money retraces the route in the opposite direction heading back to Mexico.

In the years before the crystal methamphetamine (a form of methamphetamine produced when meth in powder form is processed with acetone) produced by Mexican cartels made its way through the Atlanta region into homes in states such as Georgia and North Carolina and Virginia, in the small towns and rural communities in suburban and rural counties on the west side of Atlanta there were homegrown labs producing smaller quantities of meth powder and paste for local consumption. To this day driving through some poorer residential neighborhoods you can still see a home with a swing set in the yard next door to another home with piles of discarded trash overflowing a front porch onto a lawn that looks more like a garbage dump. The latter are the homes of people whose methamphetamine use has made them fearful of the black helicopters they believe are flying overhead and spying on them, the people hiding behind the trees in their backyard, people who are afraid of the cameras and recording devices they are sure are hidden in the television sets and home appliances they eventually rip apart and throw on their lawn trying to find the devices they believe are monitoring their lives.

Today state and local public safety and public health officials in west Georgia are well aware of the problem of methamphetamine coming from Mexico through Texas into the Atlanta area for further distribution and sales. They have been watching and studying the movement and designing and developing programs and interagency organizations like task forces to address it. When we were in west Georgia to study methamphetamine markets we talked with a group of law enforcement officers and officials. During the late twentieth century methamphetamine in western Georgia was mostly being produced and distributed by local cooks through local labs. The local cooks used traditional methods and made small quantities that they sold to small numbers of people around them. Then local law enforcement officers started to see things change around 2005, when new laws made it more difficult to purchase a key ingredient needed for making meth, pseudoephedrine, from nearby pharmacies.

As noted earlier, by design Atlanta is a hub for legitimate commerce. And according to one of the police officers, just as it is well suited for the transportation of legitimate products it is similarly well suited for the transportation of illegitimate products. Describing the Atlanta area as a place where "major interstates are like the spokes of a bicycle going out in different directions," he recalled the movement of illicit drugs such as cocaine and marijuana through the area around 2000. Then when the demand for methamphetamine could no longer be met by local lab production, it was only natural that shipments coming from the west would follow the routes for other illicit drugs and come through Atlanta. As an officer from another drug enforcement unit in the area told us, "Every drug known to man dumps into Atlanta and from there it's distributed throughout the United States."

Just as methamphetamine trafficking creates health and safety problems for communities the use of methamphetamine does unpleasant things to people. During our study of methamphetamine markets we visited with a woman, a meth user, who lived in a rural community outside Atlanta. Over the years she had been using meth in the crystal form known as ice, stopped using it, started again, then stopped again. She originally started using with her husband, from whom she has since been divorced. They had children together, but as a result of their use of the drug the children were taken from them. They also had an automobile repair business, but that too is gone. Originally they were using powder meth, but eventually they switched to ice when it started coming in from Mexico. We met with her during a time that she was not using and she told us about what her use of the drug had done to her:

> It was rough. I have a hard time remembering anything. My kidneys are messed up. My liver is messed up. I have really high liver enzymes. I had thyroid trouble since this. Sometimes I feel like I get real paranoid like somebody is trying to talk to me about stuff. I have been up so long that I've seen the Grim Reaper standing in the woods. And I have noticed some people that have done it, they see things and stuff. But then when they come back to reality they still start having those visions and stuff, and they're real paranoid, like schizophrenic people.

And the drug does not stop having its way with her even when she is not using it. She went on to tell us, "I still have cravings, some days worse than others. If I get real upset or depressed, that's when I want to go and use." She acknowledged that using meth or even having used meth has caused her a great deal of pain. And the pain was not only hers, but her family's as well.

What is methamphetamine? What do we know about it and how do we know what we think we know? How have federal and state policymakers and local law enforcement and public health officials as well as the vast majority of people living in communities across America who do not use methamphetamine responded to its presence in their lives? In this chapter we address those questions to provide a broader perspective for our study about methamphetamine use and markets. We use that background as a context for our discussion of how and why we went about trying to learn about the methamphetamine industry in

America and what we learned in the regions and communities we visited and the people we met and spoke with regarding their experience with methamphetamine.

WHAT IS METHAMPHETAMINE, WHAT DOES IT DO, AND WHAT HAVE WE AS A NATION DONE?

When chemical substances we call drugs are ingested they work their way through the body to the brain where they can alter the signals the brain is trying to send from one nerve cell to another and thereby the transmission of messages from the brain to the body to let the body know what it should do. Sometimes this is considered a good thing, as when the result is that the drug helps the body fight disease, and other times it is not. The problem is that there is not always consensus about when the effect should be considered beneficial or at least benign and when it should be considered harmful. So in all nations there are questions and concerns and policies and practices with regard to what drugs should be deemed acceptable and what drugs should not. In the United States and in each of its states, for example, there are specific laws about what drugs can be used for what purposes by which people and under what circumstances. Under these laws in some places there are some drugs that are considered to have no recognizable value for anyone under any circumstance and therefore are always and indisputably denied legal status. Yet there are, nonetheless, people who are attracted to those drugs, so industries operating outside of the law have arisen to supply the demand for them despite the fact that, under the law, they can never be sold, possessed, or used.

According to the National Institute on Drug Abuse, as a chemical substance methamphetamine is a central nervous system stimulant that both releases and blocks the reuptake of dopamine in the brain, resulting in a sense of intense euphoria for the person who uses it (National Institute on Drug Abuse 2013). It was first synthesized in 1919 in Japan for use as a nasal decongestant and for the treatment of hay fever and common colds. It reached the United States during the 1930s, was distributed to soldiers during World War II to keep them attentive and watchful, and gained popularity during the 1950s among people who viewed it as a means to stay alert or to control their weight, including athletes, truck drivers, and college students. Then during the 1960s it gained a following as a recreational drug.

Around that time concerns arose about potential risks to personal health and safety from the use of methamphetamine. In 1965, in an interview with a reporter for *the Los Angeles Free Press,* an underground newspaper, the popular Beat poet and acknowledged user of a variety of illicit drugs Allen Ginsberg warned that "speed kills," speed being a word used at the time to refer to methamphetamine. Over the years scientific studies have shown that in fact there are negative physiological and psychological consequences of using methamphetamine for the health and well-being of users and other people around them. For example, among users research has found physiological effects including cardiovascular problems, emaciation, and neurological damage as well as psychological effects including anxiety and paranoia. Similarly, research has shown negative impacts on the personal and family life of users in terms of their inability to obtain or hold a job and their experience with child neglect and domestic violence. The Drug Abuse and Regulation Control Act was passed in 1970 and set standards for keeping records and securing the quality of pharmaceuticals, including methamphetamine. By the middle of the 1970s methamphetamine use and trade seemed to be on the decline in the United States.

If there was a decline in methamphetamine use related to growing concerns for personal health and safety it was not deep or long lasting. In the mid-twentieth century heroin was a focus of media, policy, and public attention, as was crack cocaine in the later years of the century. So it is not surprising that, as was concluded in a report on drugs and drug research by the National Institute of Justice in 2003, much of the public interest in and research on illicit drug markets has been directed at crack cocaine or heroin, and much of that has been concerned with retail rather than wholesale markets. By the early years of the twenty-first century, however, attention shifted to methamphetamine as a public health and safety concern. For example, in the United States a Methamphetamine Interagency Task Force was formed in 1996 and a report in 2000 by its Federal Advisory Committee concluded that the nation was experiencing a dramatic increase in the use of methamphetamine as the drug was spreading from western states to the Midwest and the South.

During the 1990s interest in methamphetamine grew as small clandestine laboratories for making meth sprung up mostly in rural areas of the country, and mostly in the West. This attracted the interest not only of public health and safety policymakers and practitioners but also of researchers such as Denise Herz and Ralph Weisheit who increasingly began to study methamphetamine markets. Through their research and through government reports, such as the annual Threat Assessments of the National Drug Intelligence Center, we learned that local cooks in Western states and rural areas in the Midwest were busy mixing small batches of chemicals that were easily obtainable from local pharmacies and hardware stores and making enough methamphetamine to supply local consumers. These so-called mom-and-pop operations dominated the local markets and became a growing concern for public health and safety, and for the damage they were doing to the environment. In response the federal government and a number of state governments passed laws to limit access to the precursor ingredients needed to make methamphetamine, notably chemicals like pseudoephedrine and phenylpropanolamine, which were easily obtainable by purchasing common cold medications over the counter in pharmacies and neighborhood supermarkets. Congress passed the Combat Methamphetamine Epidemic Act of 2005 (Title VII of the USA PATRIOT Improvement and Reauthorization Act of 2005, P.L. 109–177), an act that specifically regulated and controlled the sale of the precursor chemicals needed to make methamphetamine. The idea was to make it at least more difficult for local cooks to manufacture methamphetamine.

The legislation and programmatic efforts to control the sale of precursor chemicals and interfere with the operation of mom-and-pop local lab methamphetamine businesses did disrupt production by local meth cooks. But, as was well known to law enforcement officers and officials in the communities where there were local meth labs and to researchers such as Duane McBride who studied the impact of the legislation, it certainly did not end the methamphetamine trade. Entrepreneurial local cooks found ways to stay in business. For example, on the local level they essentially collectivized their methamphetamine production, having meth consumers buy what precursor drugs they could under the law and giving them to the cook who would then combine the precursor drugs to prepare a batch of meth that would be shared by members of the collective. In later chapters we describe this activity in more detail in the words of the people we met during our site visits, all of whom called this activity "smurfing."

Perhaps more significant for the endurance of the methamphetamine trade in the United States, however, was the expanded importation of methamphetamine into regions and communities by large drug businesses operating predominantly out of Mexico. According to a report from the National Drug Intelligence Center in 2011, after the legislative initiatives were passed high-purity methamphetamine became more prevalent in the United States through production and distribution networks based in Mexico and Asia. Around the turn of the century and continuing to the present, government policymakers, local public health and safety officials, researchers, and even journalists agree that to a large extent illicit drugs distributed and consumed in the United States have been either manufactured in Mexico or transported through Mexico. According to the 2011 National Drug Threat Assessment, "Mexican-based TCOs [transnational criminal organizations] and their associates dominate the supply and wholesale distribution of most illicit drugs in the United States [this statement was italicized in the original]. These organizations control much of the production, transportation, and wholesale distribution of illicit drugs destined for and in the United States." On October 11, 2012, an Associated Press (AP) news story, "Cartels Flood US with Cheap Meth," by Jim Salter that was carried in newspapers all across the country reported on a recent U.S. Drug Enforcement Administration (DEA) estimate that 80 percent of methamphetamine sold in the United States was coming from or through Mexico and that the methamphetamine coming from Mexico was 90 percent pure (Salter 2012). According to the AP article, "Mexican drug cartels are quietly filling the void in the nation's drug market created by the long effort to crack down on American-made methamphetamine, flooding U.S. cities with exceptionally cheap, extraordinarily potent meth from factory-like 'superlabs.'" The article goes on to say that in Mexico methamphetamine is being produced "on an industrial scale."

As reported by journalists and researchers studying the drug trade in Mexico, such as Jerry Langton and Malcolm Beith, in the middle of the 1990s most of the Mexican drug cartels were busy transporting cocaine into the United States and considered methamphetamine to be too small in volume and too low in profit to be worth their effort, leaving the manufacture and distribution of methamphetamine to one small Mexican cartel, the Colima Cartel. That all changed around 1997 when the leaders of the Colima Cartel were all arrested and a larger cartel, the Sinaloa Cartel, took over what proved to be a very large and lucrative methamphetamine business. According to an account by Jerry Langton, the leader of the Sinaloa Cartel, who started to call himself "El Rey de Cristal" or the Crystal King, recognized the opportunity and became enamored by the methamphetamine business because meth "could be manufactured easily in huge amounts with ingredients commonly sold in pharmacies and hardware stores," meaning that he "owed nothing to the Colombians." As with the story of smurfing, in later chapters we describe in more detail through the words of the people we spoke to all over America the story of how local and regional markets that are supplied by methamphetamine from Mexico are organized and how they operate.

On the retail level, all illicit drug markets are social organizations that operate to facilitate commercial transactions involving substances that have no recognized status under the law. But markets for different illicit drugs are not all the same. For example, as researchers such as Henry Brownstein and Dana Hunt have found, methamphetamine markets are not organized or operated like crack cocaine markets. As a commodity, crack cocaine and methamphetamine are surprisingly similar. Several scholars studying crack cocaine distribution and trade in urban communities in the late twentieth century concluded that as a commercial product crack is "easy to manufacture, [can] be packaged in low-priced units for sale, and [has] high addiction potential." The same can be said for methamphetamine, though safety during manufacture may be a bit more problematic. But despite the similarity between the drugs as commercial products, the markets for local retail distribution are notably dissimilar. As a large number of studies by many researchers, including Paul Goldstein, Henry Brownstein, Philippe Bourgois, Bruce Johnson, Tom Mieczkowski, and Terry Williams, have shown, for much of the late twentieth century crack cocaine transactions embodied the public image of an open air drug market with buyers approaching strangers on street corners to exchange money for drugs. During the same period a body of studies by researchers such as Dana Hunt, Ralph Weisheit, and Rebecca McKetin has shown that methamphetamine markets largely were run like small mom-and-pop businesses out of homes and away from major roadways; even as they evolve in the twenty-first century they continue to involve buyers and sellers transacting only with people they know and trust.

WHAT DO WE KNOW ABOUT THE
METHAMPHETAMINE INDUSTRY?

In the United States methamphetamine is a controlled substance and methamphetamine markets are illicit enterprises. Consequently there are no public records of methamphetamine transactions, no reports on adherence to government regulations, and no documented accounts of revenue, earnings, or tax liability. There are no official records of the volume of production or the number of businesses operating in the United States for the manufacture or sale of methamphetamine, wholesale or retail. There are no official records of the number or characteristics of people who use methamphetamine. There are no records of how much people use it and no records of what they pay or are willing to pay for methamphetamine. So what do we know about the methamphetamine industry in America and how do we know it?

In the absence of any official documentation, what we know about the activity and productivity of methamphetamine markets or the methamphetamine industry or the value and the quality of methamphetamine in America is derived from surrogate measures. As noted earlier, statistics are extracted from data sources such as surveys of the general population and drug treatment center populations and records of law enforcement activity involving arrests of methamphetamine users and dealers, criminal prosecutions, and methamphetamine seizures and undercover purchases. These are reported to policymakers and the public by government agencies such as the National Drug Intelligence Center or by researchers and statisticians such as Jonathan Caulkins and William Rhodes. So our official knowledge of the scope and nature of the methamphetamine business in the United States comes from calculations using proxies for the things we really want to measure but are not able to measure.

Statisticians, economists, epidemiologists, and other social scientists have turned to several specific sources of data to calculate the size of the various illicit drug industries in the United States. They focus both on estimates of consumption, such as the number of known users of different drugs and how much they use, and estimates of the known supply of drugs in circulation, such as the amount of a particular drug seized by law enforcement. One main source of consumption data is national surveys of the general population, most notably the National Survey of Drug Use and Health. This is an annual nationwide household survey

produced for the federal government by the Substance Abuse and Mental
Health Services Administration. It is administered to a random sample of
seventy thousand respondents age twelve and older asking them about
their use of and experience with various illicit drugs. Another source
used to estimate consumer demand has been the Treatment Episode Data
Set, also maintained by the Substance Abuse and Mental Health Services
Administration, which reports on the drug treatment and drug using
experiences of about 1.5 million people admitted to drug treatment in a
given year. To estimate drug use based on a population known to include
a disproportionate number of heavy drug users, at least one economist,
William Rhodes, has worked with data from interviews and urine samples involving arrestee respondents.

Data for supply side estimates have come from sources including
law enforcement and criminal justice data. For example, one source is
the Uniform Crime Reports, a national and annual accounting by the
Federal Bureau of Investigation (FBI) of crimes known to the police and
arrests made by police in those known cases. A more direct source of
numbers for supply estimates of the amount of product in the country
involves calculations based on data collected by the Drug Enforcement
Administration for its System to Retrieve Information from Drug Evidence (STRIDE) program, which produces data by having laboratories
analyze drugs seized by law enforcement and submitted to DEA for this
purpose. In addition, the El Paso Intelligence Center was established by
the DEA in 1974 to collect and disseminate tactical intelligence for law
enforcement agencies involved in dealing with drug trafficking, particularly across the border with Mexico. The El Paso Intelligence Center is
not a source of new operational or accounting data, but it has been a
source for compiled data that could be used to produce illicit drug supply estimates.

Reports to the public specifically on the estimates of illicit drug production or supply and use or consumption are not produced on an annual
basis, but there have been periodic calculations and reports. William
Rhodes and his colleagues produced a report for the Office of National
Drug Control Policy on what Americans annually spent on illegal drugs
during the 1990s using many of the data sources noted above. They determined that in 2000 Americans spent $1.6 billion for methamphetamine,
down from $2.4 billion in 1989, for reasons that were not explained.

The National Drug Intelligence Center (NDIC) produces regular intelligence assessments designed for policy and practitioner audiences, and annually publishes its Threat Assessment report summarizing findings for the public. Using numbers reported through EPIC, NDIC concluded in its 2011 report that methamphetamine seizures declined along the U.S. border with Mexico in 2007 then increased "every year since" with most of the increase going into or through California. According to the 2011 NDIC report, in 2009 of the total U.S. population age twelve or older 0.5 percent reportedly had used methamphetamine during the past year and in 2010 there were 8,699 kilograms of methamphetamine seized within the United States. A report prepared for ONDCP by Arthur Fries on price and purity looked at NDIC and STRIDE estimates of the price of drugs in different cities and showed that in 2005 and 2006 the price of methamphetamine varied in selected U.S. cities from $3,500 to $11,000 per pound. Using those numbers for a simple calculation of the value of just the amount of methamphetamine removed from the markets by DEA seizure in a given year (8,699 kilograms or 19,138 pounds) the annual total amount of all methamphetamine in the country based on the DEA estimate would be worth between $66,983,000 and $210,518,000 wholesale.

Working with the consumption data, 0.5 percent of the 235 million people age eighteen or older counted in the U.S. Census in 2010 (there is no Census count reported for the number of people twelve and over) would be 1,175,000 people. If in fact they were all methamphetamine users and each used one gram per day for two days per week (the average based on the Treatment Episode Data Set and our interviews with methamphetamine users around the country) they would each use about 114 grams per year. This would come to 133,950 kilograms (or 295,226 pounds) of methamphetamine used by all methamphetamine users in the nation in one year. At $7,000 per pound (a midrange estimate from the STRIDE and NDIC city estimates) the value of the demand for methamphetamine in wholesale dollars in one year in the United States would be $2.7 billion. But regular users do not buy pounds. Regular methamphetamine users buy small quantities for personal use, such as grams or "eight balls" (an eighth of an ounce). So the almost $3 billion estimate for the value of methamphetamine sold in America, assuming it is anywhere near accurate, would be far exceeded by the number of dollars methamphetamine users actually would be exchanging for the amount of methamphetamine they consume. We recognize that estimating the commercial value of the illicit methamphetamine industry in the United States in this way is overly simplistic. But no matter how simple or sophisticated the analysis, given available data sources, the diversity of policy and program interests, and the limitations of contemporary statistical and analytic methods, any attempt to accurately estimate the economy of an illicit drug market is challenging if not impossible. Nonetheless, given all that is known it seems safe to say that annually methamphetamine is a multibillion dollar industry in the United States. That is, the methamphetamine industry in America is big business.

HOW WE STUDIED THE METHAMPHETAMINE INDUSTRY IN AMERICA

When we first became interested in learning about methamphetamine markets and the methamphetamine industry in America we started by reading everything we could find on the subject. We read government agency reports, books and articles based on research others had conducted, and even news accounts by print and electronic reporters and journalists. Because the methamphetamine business in America was changing with traditional local mom-and-pop labs meeting growing competition from larger corporate producers and distributors, we quickly realized that we would need to take a broader national view of the business as an industry if we hoped to understand it. But we also recognized that we would need to look deeper into local regions and communities in order to appreciate the dynamics of local retail markets in the context of the national and even international industry. So our study was designed to incorporate a national perspective with a local orientation. In an appendix at the end of this book we describe our study in greater detail with more attention to the technical elements. Below we present a brief overview of the study to provide a framework for readers to understand what we did, what we learned, the source of our findings, and how and why we reached our conclusions.

From 2007 to 2011 we conducted a study of the dynamics of methamphetamine markets with funding from a grant from the National Institute on Drug Abuse (NIDA Grant Number R21DA024391). It was clear from our reading that local markets were inevitably and inextricably connected in one way or another to the larger national industry; to understand them we would need to know what kinds of markets there were and where they were located and then to be able to closely examine those markets through the eyes of the people directly involved with them. So we designed an exploratory study using a mixture of both quantitative and qualitative research methods integrated in a way that would best help us to search for information that would allow us to best understand the markets. The quantitative methods would be useful for counting things about markets so we could distinguish markets in different places by different characteristics. The qualitative methods would be useful for probing deeper into the meanings of the things people told us and the things we observed in the stories and experience of people and communities where there were active local methamphetamine markets.

The first stage of our study was an information-gathering screening survey of 1,367 police agencies from all fifty states. We chose to survey police agencies not because they are the only source of information about methamphetamine markets but because they are the one organization in every community that has an explicit mandate to locate and respond to illicit activity, including illicit drug markets. That is, police agencies are uniquely well situated to know something about local methamphetamine markets. Each of the agencies responding to the survey provided information about methamphetamine use and markets in their jurisdiction, where the drug came from, how and where it was being sold, how it related to local public safety and health problems, and how methamphetamine was produced, sold, purchased, and used in the area. From the survey we learned what different markets in different places had in common and how they were different. The greatest variation was found between markets based on local lab production and those based on methamphetamine imported from Mexico. Using these data we were then able to identify fifty police agencies for the next stage of our study, open-ended and in-depth telephone interviews.

The telephone interviews were conducted with narcotics detectives from fifty police agencies in communities selected from those that had responded to the survey. So before we ever called or even approached our respondents we had already communicated with officials in the agency, explained the aim of our study, and established an agreement to conduct the interview. Based on analysis of our survey data, the fifty communities represented areas with different types of meth markets and different levels of problems with methamphetamine. The purpose of the interview was to gain a deeper understanding of how local markets were organized and operated and how they related to the national industry. To enhance the capacity of our respondents to take us deeper into the local story of methamphetamine and methamphetamine markets, the interviews all included not only a telephonic connection but also a connection through a web-based conferencing software program (WebEx) that allowed the interviewer and the respondent to share written, graphic, and symbolic images. Through this connection we provided access to Google maps geocoded with the specific locations of all seizures by the Drug Enforcement Administration over five years, allowing us to share an image of a map of the area where the respondent was located and to use that map interactively to locate and discuss specific methamphetamine-related activity in the jurisdiction. Each interview lasted from one to two hours, and from them we learned more about the organization and operation of local methamphetamine markets. Using these findings we selected five regions of the country for the next stage of our study, site visits to places where it would be most informative and productive to observe community activity and talk to people about local methamphetamine markets and the national industry.

The data from the telephone interviews helped us to distinguish specific regions and communities where through observations and open-ended, in-person interviews we would be able to learn about the social experience of people involved with methamphetamine markets in different types and mixes of markets. Since our contacts with police were already well established, the police served as our hosts and guides in communities in each of the five regions. Through them we were introduced to other respondents who in turn introduced us to others. We spoke with a wide range of people who were participants in or knowledgeable about local methamphetamine market activity including regional public health and safety officials, drug treatment and family service providers, drug prevention program workers, meth users and dealers, meth cooks, and others. Over the period of about one year we visited more than twenty-eight cities and towns and rural communities in five regions of the country (Southeast, Middle Atlantic, Midwest, Southwest, and Pacific Northwest). Spending a week or more in each we walked or drove through areas where local people told us that methamphetamine was being produced or being bought and sold and places where we were told we would find buildings and homes either belonging to or being used by methamphetamine users and dealers. We also attended community events and listened to local people talking about the impact of methamphetamine on their community. In the Southwest we were given a tour of the U.S.-Mexico border by a member of the U.S. Border Patrol.

GOING FORWARD

Our nationwide study identified different types and mixes of methamphetamine markets. Some areas had no known methamphetamine markets to report while others had newly emerging markets where none had existed before. From our analyses of our survey and interview data, supported by our site visits, we observed two main types of markets. We found places with methamphetamine markets built around production in local, homegrown mom-and-pop labs where a local cook would use a simple yet dangerous technique to produce enough reasonably good but usually not great quality methamphetamine for him or herself (usually himself) to use while having some left over to sell to or share with a few other people he or she knows. No one was getting rich, but good cooks could make enough meth to stay high and earn enough money to support themselves with a modest livelihood. We also found markets where, rather than being made locally, the methamphetamine supply in the local market was imported, mostly from Mexico but sometimes from other places like California where Mexican producers had opened production facilities. In these import markets the product is crystal meth, arguably better quality, but always more refined and better looking. The crystal meth is delivered to the area in larger quantities and distributed through local representatives of the production organization but sold at the community level through local retail dealers selling small amounts to people they know or with whom they are at least familiar. Some areas we found had predominantly one type of market, others had both. We found that areas with both mom-and-pop and import markets were more likely to report related public health and safety problems than those with just one type of market, though rarely did we hear about violence being directly associated with the organization or operation of methamphetamine markets as such. In the world of methamphetamine users the more serious problems of meth-related violence and neglect were found in families. In summary, we learned how the methamphetamine industry in America is organized and operates nationwide in relation to an international industry dominated by Mexican drug organizations often called cartels. To understand and explain methamphetamine markets it is necessary to study them as part of and integrally related not only to the local and regional community but also to the national and international industries.

Perhaps our most important finding is that in the early twenty-first century in the United States, in many but not all communities, methamphetamine is a thriving industry and a serious problem for public health, public safety, and the local economy. Federal and state legislation designed to address meth-related problems initially did inconvenience the marketers of methamphetamine, but it also had unintended outcomes that revitalized the methamphetamine industry. In the following chapters we share what we learned directly from the people we spoke to both on the telephone and in person about the story of how methamphetamine markets in America are organized and operate as part of a much larger industry and how the industry and markets evolved over the last years of the first decade of the twenty-first century in response to public policy efforts to shut them down. In particular, we tell the story in terms of the structure of social activity, the nature of social relationships, and cultural forms and patterns of the markets and the industry as viewed through the personal experience of the people whose lives intersect with methamphetamine use and methamphetamine markets.

CHAPTER 3

Social Activity in the Methamphetamine Industry

THE ONE-POT or shake-and-bake technique is a popular method for small-scale meth cooks. One-pot is no less, and maybe even more, dangerous than other methods and with it you can make only a small amount of meth. But one-pot has become popular in communities with small local labs because it is a simpler process that requires only one person to do the cooking, no heating, and a smaller quantity of pseudoephedrine (an ingredient in cold tablets used in making meth). In a two-liter bottle, the kind in which you would buy soda pop, the cook mixes all the ingredients together following the correct sequence and timing to make sure that nothing goes wrong. Then the bottle is shaken, gas is slowly released from the bottle (very carefully so that it does not explode), and finally the finished product is ready to be shared. The cook is ready to sit down with the small group of people who may have each brought what cold pills they could buy and are waiting for the cook to get done. Then they share the product and get high together. This is a social activity involving one cook and a few people he or she knows who together are engaged in a common if not intimate social experience.

One-pot is not the only way to make methamphetamine. For both large and small scale production there are different ways to make meth. Other methods may involve a cooking process that requires more people working together or may have the capacity to produce larger quantities for a greater number of people who will be using the finished product. Ralph Weisheit, a criminologist known for his studies of methamphetamine in rural communities, concluded that historically there have been two main methods for producing methamphetamine differentiated by the precursor or foundation drug used in the processing. The phenyl-2-propanone method, known as P2P, was popular among motorcycle gangs producing and selling a lower quality methamphetamine in the western parts of the United States until around 1980 when the gangs lost control of the meth markets, P2P became a regulated drug in the United States, and other methods became more popular as new groups of consumers discovered better products. This method uses P2P and a derivative of ammonia called methylamine as the primary precursor drugs and also uses a number of other chemicals such as hydrochloric acid, formic acid, or mercury. Because the process is time consuming and involves serious laboratory equipment, it is useful for larger scale production as might be found today in the superlabs of Mexican cartels.

The other popular method for making methamphetamine is a technique known as the ephedrine/pseudoephedrine reduction method. This is a simpler method and involves relatively inexpensive household products. For local mom-and-pop labs this became the more popular method of production in the United States at the end of the twentieth century. Ephedrine or pseudoephedrine is converted to methamphetamine by reducing an oxygen molecule using methods known as the red phosphorous or Red-P method or the Nazi or Birch method. The Red-P method uses red phosphorous to make the conversion and the Nazi method uses anhydrous ammonia and chemicals such as lithium from batteries, lye, and paint thinner.

In April 2013 members of our research team were called by a reporter for jconline.com, a Gannett Company online version of the *Journal and Courier* in Lafayette, Indiana. Emily Campion was writing a story about methamphetamine production in Indiana and was wondering why the number of lab seizures was so high in the state. According to the DEA in 2012 there were 1,429 seizures in Indiana, the third most in the country. From us and several other people she interviewed for the article, which was published on April 19, 2013, she learned about one-pot meth cooking and how easy it is for seizures to add up when any number of them might simply be a single soda bottle on the side of the road. In the article she described what she had learned: "Producers don't have to look far to find what they need: camp fuel, lithium batteries, drain cleaner, decongestant, assorted other chemicals and a 16-ounce plastic bottle. Methods of cooking meth have evolved from fairly bulky setups to portable labs that can fit into a duffel bag, travel bag or even a coat pocket." She labeled another section of the article with the subheading "Indiana an 'anomaly'"

(Campion 2013). For better or worse Indiana may be different from states in other parts of the country, but in the Midwest it is one of many states faced with a similar circumstance. As we learned from our study, the Midwest, with its growing number of one-pot local labs and little or no imported methamphetamine, is different.

When we traveled through Midwestern states such as Illinois, Kentucky, Missouri and Indiana, we learned that methamphetamine production remains largely a local industry. Mom-and-pop businesses supply the local demand for methamphetamine with little or no competition from the import conglomerates operated by the Mexican cartels in many other parts of the country. This is interesting because the meth producers from Mexico operate large corporate-type organizations that have great capacity, reach, and power and there are interstate highways and rivers and world-class airports in the region that make transportation of the finished product possible. Perhaps the explanation can be found in the legend of Bob Paillet, arguably the Johnny Appleseed for the spread of local meth production throughout the Midwest.

The *Springfield News-Leader,* a Gannett newspaper in Springfield, Missouri, ran a story on August 3, 2007, called "'Nazi Dope': Meth Reinvented in the Ozarks" (*Springfield News-Leader* staff 2007). According to the story, Bob Paillet is "something of a legend" for his "role in propagating what is known as the Nazi dope method" throughout the region. During the 1990s Paillet moved to Springfield from California and found the local meth to be more expensive and less accessible than West Coast meth. Despite lacking a background in chemistry he went to the library at Southwest Missouri State University where he read lots of books and learned about the methamphetamine made during World War II by the Nazis to keep "appetites down, spirits up and adrenaline rushing" among German soldiers. Once he figured out the method they had used, "He taught all his buddies how to do it, they taught all their buddies to do it, and now it's out of control." Looking back, a local police official is quoted as saying, "I never thought it would spread like this."

When we visited towns and cities throughout the Midwest region for our study of methamphetamine markets one of our stops was Jacksonville, Illinois, where we spoke with local law enforcement officers and officials. Jacksonville is in southern Illinois, closer to St. Louis than to Chicago. The county seat of Morgan County, Jacksonville is a small city with a population of 19,446 people, according to the 2010 Census. Almost all of the people who live there consider themselves to be rural dwellers, and about 80 percent of residents are white with just a few hundred people who identify themselves as Hispanic. The city is named for Andrew Jackson (before he was elected president) and Abraham Lincoln spent some time there representing clients in the County Courthouse. Jacksonville is much like many other places we visited in the Midwest. Jacksonville, like Indiana, is not an anomaly.

One police respondent in Jacksonville told us about meth production in his area, including his version of the legend of Bob Paillet. What he told us helps explain the spread of the home cooking of methamphetamine and the current situation with meth production in the region:

> It's constantly evolving, and constantly changing. Now the big thing is the one-pot method. When I was here in the '90s, there were the Nazi dope labs, which were using the pseudoephedrine with lithium metal and anhydrous ammonia. And it was a different process than the one-pot method. It doesn't make as much methamphetamine at one time, but it's a lot quicker and a lot easier to do. That being said, it's also a lot more dangerous. A little bit of the history of how it transformed: In the 1980s I was assigned to the southwest portion of Missouri with [a federal agency]. We covered thirty-six counties in the southwest corner, including Springfield. And back then we had the larger P2P labs and also the red phosphorous iodine labs. . . . It completely changed course in the early 1990s, and that's when the actual explosion occurred with the Nazi dope. And there was a fella by the name of Bob Paillet. Robert Paillet moved from San Diego, California, first to Kansas City and then settled down in Springfield. And he brought with him this Nazi dope method of manufacturing methamphetamine. The method's been around a long time, it just wasn't being used. . . . [When he got arrested] he actually gave a confession to DEA, where they taped it. He sold this recipe, as he called it, to hundreds and hundreds of people, including in the Kansas City area. And that slowly moved from west to east, and it didn't hit Illinois, actually, the first Nazi dope lab we did in Illinois was in May of 1997. . . . That was the start of it here in Illinois. Then it just spread like wildfire across the state going to Indiana going south into Kentucky, Tennessee, etc.

His telling of the legend may be a bit different, but the story is the same. It is a story of the social activity through which people living in an area learned to produce and continue to produce methamphetamine for personal use.

The point of all this is that methamphetamine markets are social organizations involving the social activity of people as they relate to each other to get things done. In the methamphetamine industry this activity would include things like how people can and should produce the product they are making and how they can or should distribute it both across regions and within communities in order for production and distribution to be successful. In society social activity and social relations are shaped by normative patterns of behavior, forming organizations and institutions that serve as a foundation or framework for not only civil but also productive social life. These organizations and institutions structure activity in a way that provides guidance for people, showing them how to act in relation to others around them in order to accomplish what they are trying to accomplish. The objective in the methamphetamine industry is to make a product that people will want to use and to get it to them so the user can use it and the producer can profit from its use.

Generations of sociologists and anthropologists, including theorists such as Emile Durkheim and Max Weber and A. R. Radcliffe-Brown, have referred to this property of social life in their writings about norms (those abstract patterns that set standards or limits for socially reputable or at least decorous behavior) and social institutions (those distinctive complexes of behavior patterns that normalize and even regulate social activity). As prescribed or proscribed standards for routine patterns of behavior, social norms and institutions guide social activity and comportment in the methamphetamine industry and its markets as they are observed and experienced through the means and methods of production, distribution, and use of methamphetamine.

METHAMPHETAMINE PRODUCTION AS SOCIAL ACTIVITY

During the period of our study between 2007 and 2011 we found evidence of two models of methamphetamine production serving U.S. markets: (1) indigenous mom-and-pop labs where a local cook would produce a small amount of meth to supply local consumers, and (2) superlabs where larger quantities of a different quality were produced for export to serve local users in any number of local markets. Of the 1,367 police departments surveyed for our study, 292 (21 percent) reported that there were no methamphetamine markets in their area. Of the remaining 1,075 departments with acknowledged markets, 194 (18 percent) reported only one type of meth market in their area while the others reported more than one type. That is, where markets were acknowledged about one of every five communities served by these departments had either only local labs (11 percent of 1,075) or only imported meth (7 percent). All other places were experiencing a mix of both types. From our interviews and site visits we were able to learn how methamphetamine was being produced for both local lab and import markets.

As noted earlier, in the later twentieth century the methamphetamine industry in America was dominated by local producers operating what were often called mom-and-pop labs. And while cooking meth may be dangerous and there may be more difficulty today in getting the necessary ingredients, the process is not complicated and the ingredients are still available. As a meth cook from rural Georgia explained:

> Well, what I can tell you about meth is it's a manmade product. Any local store you go to, you can pretty much buy the ingredients, whether it's the lithium batteries they use now, the lye that you pour down your sink drain, Coleman fuel that you light your own camping stove, ammonium nitrate fertilizer, or just pure ammonium nitrate. You got ingredients you need in your closets to keep your clothes from getting all ruined and stuff . . . liquid smoke [used for barbecuing] . . . you can also pour it down your drains to clean them out. I mean it can eat a hole through the floor. I mean that's how bad that stuff is.

Over time the chemistry and technology for cooking meth has evolved, but normatively the social activity of the people involved in these local labs remains as it has always been. Production in local mom-and-pop labs makes enough meth to supply the cook and some number of family, friends, and acquaintances. The labs are organized and operated to produce enough meth for a small circle of people and not for widespread distribution.

Although the legislation of the early twenty-first century shuttered labs in some places and for some time, these labs continue to thrive today in certain areas of the country, including the Middle Atlantic, Southeast, Midwest, and Southwest. In some areas the local cooks continue to use traditional methods to make methamphetamine. For example, a narcotics detective in Tennessee described how meth labs in his area continue to use the Nazi method: "Pretty much about all of our labs are what you call Nazi labs, and it's where they use anhydrous ammonia. So far, as far as this new method of business goes, we've only seen a couple or three of those here, but I'm figuring we're going to be working more and more of those." The new method he was talking about was shake-and-bake. A narcotics detective from a larger city in Ohio described how the local labs in his area evolved as the technology and chemistry for making methamphetamine changed over the years:

> About ten to fifteen years ago, we did a couple of meth cases where they were making larger quantities and now with the new method of manufacturing, first there was a P2P [phenyl-2-propanone] method, then there was a red phosphorus method, and both of those entailed several hours and a little bit of know-how. And of course they have this Nazi method which takes only two or three hours and it's a little less complicated. We're seeing smaller quantities when it comes to manufacturing, like someone just cooking an ounce of meth as opposed to a pound.

The recipes and technology may have changed, but neither one ounce nor even one pound is sufficient for widespread distribution, though it can support some number of local users.

Respondents from other areas offered similar descriptions of evolving methods used by mom-and-pop labs for producing relatively small quantities of meth. For example, a detective in Georgia told us: "Once the cooks used predominantly the Nazi method, but now we're seeing a different method which is called the cold method. They use freezer packs from Walmart to do what they call 'shake-and-bake.' It's a one-bottle operation now. You don't need separate bottles. You just put everything in one bottle." Arguably making it even easier for shake-and-bake cooks, local legitimate retail stores seem to be making sure that the cooks have access to all the freezer packs they need. A police official in Missouri told us: "Walk into a Dollar General Store and you'll see a whole section of ice packs. Dollar General Stores in our area are the biggest precursor apparatus sellers because they know." He told us that this local store never carried ice packs before the growth in local mom-and-pop meth labs, but now they were stacking the packs in the front of the store.

A detective from a small town in Arkansas described the shake-and-bake method used in his area. What he told us suggests how even with the changes in technique for making meth, the social activity of the people involved in the mom-and-pop labs in his area continues to be organized to serve a small number of known users.

> They got a new technique of cooking meth and it's just called cold cook method. It's called shake-and-bake. That's how most of the people that are doing the mom-and-pop labs now, and these are people who they're really down on their luck; they have very little money. They're claiming to be an addict; they can't get off of it. Pretty much that whole circle, anybody who's been arrested, they all know each other. It's just one big circle. Some people are in different cliques to where they can still get dope from different people, but they all pool their resources and buy as many packs of pseudoephedrine as they can now, if they're just doing the mom-and-pop method.

Similarly, a police respondent from South Carolina described the local labs in his area as "box labs": It was something very small. . . . In box labs they make something they could just carry in and carry out real quick. They'll stay there overnight for a day or so and cook it up and just have a girl come stay over, a couple of her friends and they do whatever they made."

A meth cook we interviewed in Georgia told us he preferred the shake-and-bake method because "it's easier than the old-style method." Also, sufficient supplies for shake-and-bake are easier to get so "it's the only method that you can really do right now. Shake-and-bake is easier, it's faster." According to his own assessment he was well trained and highly skilled. Unfortunately, the last time he cooked meth he gave in to his own sense of his expertise as a cook and his desire to satisfy his customers. By his own account he agreed after having been up for two days cooking meth and drinking alcohol to "mix six one-pot bottles at one time," resulting in an explosion and costing him not only his freedom (he was arrested) but also much of his skin, the mobility of his neck and limbs, and the loss of several of his fingers.

Local mom-and-pop meth labs, then, can be thought of as small neighborhood or town businesses with an unusually high level of risk. Whatever chemistry or technology is used by the cook, these labs are socially organized to produce small quantities of methamphetamine for local distribution to a small number of people, most if not all of whom are known to the cook. In a sense they are organized and operate like social collectives. In the Midwest, where local lab production is still the main source of methamphetamine, a detective from Missouri told us:

> My experience with one-pot cooks, they're just cookin' enough for themselves and enough to deal enough to get the next cook goin'. It's not about money. It's just about the meth and the cookin' process. It takes ten or fifteen people to bring everything together now because of all the stipulations. You gotta present ID. A cook is not gonna go out and get his own stuff. They're gonna sit in their apartment and wait for the ten or fifteen people, because it's safer for them. And they just divvy out to that circle. And they just keep doin' that.

What this produces is a near cashless economy different from what is commonly found in street corner drug markets in urban areas. Users addicted to methamphetamine trade precursors and favors to the manufacturers who operate as dealers for the finished product. One former user from Georgia who called herself an addict described her personal interactions with her meth dealer as follows: "I was going to the store. I wanted to know if she wanted something from the store because you always have to be super nice to her and clean her house, and you had to do things like that for her." This type of market operation can be particularly frustrating for law enforcement officers because of the highly decentralized nature of the market, and also because local cooks and users often lack cash or valuable assets that might be confiscated through asset forfeiture. Perhaps even of greater concern, crime scenes involving methamphetamine production contain hazardous waste. On the other hand, these local production markets are well contained and participants lack the sophistication and productivity to expand or grow outside the confines of their small locale.

In contrast, the production of methamphetamine for import markets is very different. The meth sold in import markets is produced in what are called "superlabs" and the production process is organized and operates like a large nonlocal business with a corporate structure including things like institutionalized lines of responsibility and authority and a strict focus on revenue growth and profit. In a December 4, 2010, *Wall Street Journal* article, "Meth Labs Make Return to U.S.," Justin Scheck wrote: "Illicit meth labs declined after U.S. laws curbed the availability of ingredients needed to manufacture the drug, a potent and highly addictive stimulant. As large-scale production, especially in the West, moved to Mexico, many U.S. dealers began importing Mexican meth" (Scheck 2010). At least one person in the business community was noticing the attraction of big business, even if illegal, to new opportunities to make money from the production and distribution of methamphetamine. In 2012 our research team had a number of conversations with Scheck about methamphetamine and what we were learning for a September 13, 2012, article, "Business Plan Remakes Meth Market" (Scheck 2012). In this article he quotes an agent who held the senior position in the Fresno, California, office of the U.S. Drug Enforcement Administration, John Donnelly: "The sophisticated logistics show how Mexican drug groups have developed the business expertise to adapt to changing markets and law-enforcement strategies." Scheck goes on to say, "The new model mimics legal industries that have found that, rather than importing finished products, it is more efficient to do final processing close to their customers." When we talk about the emergence of new forms of social activity in import methamphetamine markets, including the establishment of superlabs in places such as California and Arizona, this is known not only to us and the people we spoke with but also to the business and law enforcement communities in the United States.

When federal and state legislation after 2004 made it more difficult for local meth cooks to secure the chemicals (especially pseudoephedrine) needed to cook meth, the demand for meth did not go away. Illicit drug enterprises already distributing other drug products to drug users in the United States seized the opportunity and superlabs were opened to produce a large enough supply of methamphetamine for widespread wholesale distribution. Superlabs were opened in the United States, notably in California, and in Mexico for export to the United States. Not only were the superlabs a source of methamphetamine when the local lab supply was diminished, but the quality of the product was different. Local labs were mostly producing powder or paste (called "peanut butter" or "crank" by users), sometimes coloring it to make their product distinctive. Superlabs mostly produced crystal meth. The difference in quality from the user perspective varied, but they do smell and taste different and, in the main, the crystal is considered to be purer, more potent, and to have a more pleasing appearance. As a respondent from the state of Washington said, "The backyard mom-pop labs, theirs is powder. They're doing their best to make it into crystal but the purities are real low. I would say 80 percent [of meth in this area] for certain is coming from across the border, the Mexican superlabs, and it's pure crystal. It's high-quality, high-grade stuff." When the law made it more difficult for local meth cooks to obtain the necessary ingredients to produce meth, the superlabs filled the void with a new social structure to support the production of methamphetamine and, as an added bonus, they brought a newer and more attractive product to the market.

What are called superlabs are rarely labs as a scientist would think of a lab and are hardly super. They are not big factories with tall smokestacks sending toxic clouds of waste from methamphetamine production into the air. Whatever the scale of production, methamphetamine is an illicit substance so any location where production takes place needs to be concealed. Superlabs are sometimes simply oversized versions of local labs hidden in buildings, trailer parks, or single family homes where larger quantities of methamphetamine can be produced. They are intended to produce greater quantities for more widespread distribution to many markets. At the high end they produce enough to make it possible and profitable to operate and export product to other regions or even across international borders.

The import meth markets in the United States mostly get their product from superlabs in Mexico or from Mexican businesses operating superlabs in the United States. As one police respondent in Oregon told us, "the superlabs in California are all Mexican DTO [drug trafficking organization] labs." A narcotics detective from Utah described how the transition from local lab production to production in superlabs run by Mexican organizations took place.

I don't know why the pattern changed but around two or three years ago, maybe a little bit longer, Mexico really became the primary source of supply for methamphetamine in Utah. As soon as the federal laws came about and all of the local cooks in Utah, the people who were making methamphetamine, once they were slowly weeded out to the point that all of Utah was only seeing maybe ten labs a year over the past couple of years because, really, all the people who have that knowledge were weeded out. Everyone called in on their neighbor who had anything funky going on to say they had a meth lab. So labs really tanked for a long time. And so the Mexican markets absolutely took over and all meth that we dealt with came from Mexico. . . . I knew that the DEA, because they do purity tests in the San Francisco western regional laboratory, they would really tell you where it was coming from. They could tell you that that meth was not manufactured locally.

A detective from a small town in California pointed out that not all the meth produced by the big Mexican producers is manufactured in Mexico: "The biggest manufacturers we know are in Mexico, but there are also the big manufacturers in Arizona. Some of our bigger manufacturers who make meth locally, if you will, are within a radius of fifty miles or in the high desert." Thus, domestic superlab production was not limited to just one state, California.

Over time local, national, and international policies and practices change and the extent to which an illicit product like methamphetamine is produced locally in small mom-and-pop labs or internationally in super-labs varies. For example, when Mexico, like the United States, placed limits on the availability of pseudoephedrine there was a resurgence of local labs in some places in the United States. It is interesting, however, how the production methods of one type of lab will influence the production methods of the other. For example, a detective from a town in Oregon, where today pseudoephedrine products are only available by prescription, described how earlier when local cooks were still able to produce meth in Oregon they took lessons from the success of the Mexican importers. Discussing the period around 2003 to 2004 when imported crystal meth became the favorite of local users in Oregon, he said:

Everything went to ice [crystal meth], even local production, because all they need to do to turn methamphetamine into ice is to take the finished powder methamphetamine, add acetone to it, and let it evaporate off or put it in the freezer. Let it evaporate slowly and it creates ice crystal. So there's no change in the production method, whether it's the reduction method or the Nazi method. All it is is adding one more step of dropping acetone into the powder of methamphetamine, stirring it up and letting it evaporate, which creates ice. And if it's cleaned really well then it's crystal clear.

Similarly, a detective from a large city in Arizona described what he called a "wash lab," where finished product was being converted to "ice or glass."

A respondent who worked on a multijurisdictional interagency law enforcement team in Georgia described the significance of conversion labs in his area. He called the area "the armpit of the country" for the movement of "any known drug" thanks to having "so many different [transportation] routes" and "an increasing population of Mexican nationals moving to the area." The meth comes from Mexico as powder and is converted to "glass shards" or slivers in large and well-established "icing labs" that compete with meth made locally in mom-and-pop shake-and-bake labs. But, he notes, the labs converting the Mexican product can produce much greater amounts, "as much as hundreds of pounds a day." This is the level of production that is necessary to sustain production for wholesale distribution.

METHAMPHETAMINE WHOLESALE DISTRIBUTION AS SOCIAL ACTIVITY

In local mom-and-pop labs meth is produced on a small scale for local users. So the extent to which distribution can be considered wholesale is limited. Superlabs on the other hand produce meth for widespread wholesale distribution. As described by a police official in Illinois, "When you get these big labs, there's money. There's money funding them, there's money in return. With the mom-and-pop, there's not." In describing the production from superlabs, respondents not only talked about the labs themselves or the fact that they were largely organized and operated by Mexican illegal businesses but also about the fact that the methamphetamine produced in these labs was not just brought to a place and dumped. They specifically described how the meth produced in the superlabs was distributed through different forms of social activity that structured how the meth was transported and structured its wholesale distribution at the regional and local levels.

Wholesale distribution of a manufactured product, in this case meth-amphetamine, by definition involves transport of the product from the place of production to any number of consumer markets where it will be sold. Such transportation necessitates social processes and patterns for moving quantities of meth from one place to another. As respondents made clear to us, it also necessitates moving money paid by consumers for the meth back to the producers. This all has to be done in the shadow of the law, so wholesale distributors need to be resourceful and find different ways to move both meth and money.

In western parts of the country, where methamphetamine has been around longer and especially places that are closer to the Mexican border, respondents reported meth being transported in cars with specially designed hidden compartments. A meth dealer from Oregon told us that along the West Coast retrofitted cars are used to bring meth and other drugs going north, and cash going south. His family originally came from Mexico and he grew up in Los Angeles where he was a crack dealer before moving north to sell meth:

> When meth comes as a big shipment and they're going to distrib-ute it in like almost all of Portland, it comes in different cars just to spread out the potential losses. . . . The people that are here [the meth dealers], they've never done it and never use it and they just want [people not involved in the business] for a driver. And they're like, oh, man, you're going to go pick it up. He doesn't even know how much is on the car or the truck and he just goes and picks it up, he just gets paid maybe a couple of thousand dollars. They're like I'm going to give you supposedly six thousand bucks, go get that car from California and just bring it here. And he doesn't even have an idea. But then if the guy really knows what it goes for, he'll be charg-ing at least a thousand bucks per key [kilo] or per pound, whatever he got. So he'd be like if you got twenty keys [kilos], you're going to give me twenty thousand dollars for each k[ilo] that's on that car. And plus the cars are already professionally done for the dogs [to prevent trained dogs from finding the drug] and all that stuff. It costs money just to do that too. That costs a couple of thousand dollars just to fix the car. . . . A lot of people just take it in the car. Like it can be in the tank, it can be anywhere on the car. They don't give a fuck

about the car. They let the guy that's taking the car keep the car. They tell him, 'You take that car over there, the car is yours.' That's smart. They always use a different car every time they come over here. If it costs six thousand to fix the car [to make the compartment to hide the drugs or money] and they bring thirty kilos here, hey, man, that's a good deal.

In that way cars prove to be useful for transporting methamphetamine not only because the drugs can be hidden in the car but also because the arrangements that can be made with drivers protect the manufacturers and sellers from exposure to unnecessary risk.

A member of an interagency drug crime law enforcement team in rural Georgia told us about the use of cars to transport meth in his region:

A dealer who was an informant said in his organization they had three cars that were trapped out [fitted with hiding places for drugs], and they would do three trips a week to South Carolina with meth or whatever that group up there needed. It would come here to this "jefe" [chief] and then they would take orders. For the driver [of the car] you've got one expendable man. All right, here's $5,000. That guy doesn't usually know what he's doing. All he knows he's going to drive a car from here to here. He'll say, take this car and drive it to Walmart, here's a phone number. Call this guy when you get to Walmart, go inside and shop. When he's ready, somebody else will come pick up the car, put it in a trap, trap it out, drive it back to Walmart and he'll get a phone call saying the car is ready. He'll go drive this car to wherever he's got to go and that's all he knows. He doesn't know whether he's got a bomb in the back of it or money, guns, dope, whatever. He just knows he's going to drive this car from here to there and make a phone call when he gets there.

It would appear that the method used to transport methamphetamine is whatever method works.

From what we were told trucks are more commonly used to transport the product in the Southeast and Middle Atlantic regions, parts of the country where meth, especially imported meth, is a new product, and to transport cash back to Mexico. Whether it be a truck or a car, the drivers were not likely to be regular employees of the organization manufacturing and distributing the drug. The drivers, as we were told in Georgia and elsewhere, are expendable. As a narcotics detective from Arkansas described it, in his region the truck drivers are not employees of the Mexican business doing the importing. In a sense, they are more like private subcontractors: "A lot of truckers drive the Mexican ice product. A lot of individuals do that. That's what they do for a living. They come up. They have no ID, nothing. Most of them are illegal. Every now and then you'll get somebody that's local that gets in over his head and they either got a big habit or they owe a lot of money and they're asked to drive. They're white truckers. Trucker comes up, parks his truck, somebody would come get the product, distribute them up to the dealers here in town or around our community." Whether cars or trucks or even planes, trains, or buses are used, the goal of the methamphetamine industry as a social organization is to transport the meth from producers to distributors ultimately for sale to consumers and the money from consumers back to producers.

As a social organization or as a commercial enterprise the methamphetamine industry is primarily oriented to attaining its goal of delivering its product to consumers in exchange for payment. To do that it needs to use the available transportation routes effectively and efficiently. Fortunately for the people who do business in the meth industry in America, the United States has a very good system of highways that facilitates the movement of commercial goods from one place to another through a network of strategically placed depots or hubs. A drug treatment counselor from Virginia described his area as a hub because "we got this wonderful highway, it goes in every which direction." His colleague from Virginia, where the methamphetamine industry has taken root, described how this works: "Over the past four or five years the Shenandoah Valley has been kind of the hub for the East Coast for methamphetamine. . . . We're the third stop or in some cases the second stop straight from Mexico being either through Denver, Kansas City, or North Carolina in the distribution wheel there." A police respondent from Nebraska while looking at the Google map of his region during our telephone interview with him referred to specific roads, routes, and even places:

> [Route] 283 comes into Lexington and then intersects with 80 and just a mile north on the east side is where the meat packing plant is.

But 283 comes up from Garden City, Kansas, and a lot of that comes from Garden City. That's another meat packing town, and a lot of other drugs come from there up to Lexington and then it goes from Lexington down to our area and then up to Grand Island and down to Hastings even. And a lot of it comes from California on 80, from California from the Mexican cartels and Lexington and then Grand Island and Hastings and it goes to Buffalo County and down to us from there.

And even where meth markets have yet to be established, the expectation is that the product will follow the same pattern. A respondent in Illinois said: "Chicago has always been a big hub for the Midwest for the historic drugs like marijuana, cocaine, heroin, and I'm sure that when meth starts to come up in bigger quantities from the Southwest border, I'm sure Chicago would be the hub for other areas." The people who provide leadership in the methamphetamine industry know the transportation system in the United States and how to use it from their experience having done business in other illicit drug industries that over the years have operated along these same routes.

What distinguishes methamphetamine markets from many other illicit drug markets is the fact that methamphetamine transactions almost always involve people who know and trust each other, who have an established level of comfort with one another. This creates a problem for wholesale distributors who come to a region to establish businesses to supply the local markets. They need to recruit local people who are known in the community to sell their product for them to local consumers. A member of a police drug unit in the state of Washington describes how white local dealers are recruited to sell to white meth users:

Most of the [street] meth dealers that I've dealt with have been white. I have not dealt with many black meth dealers. The Hispanics, some, but I don't see it on the street level so much. When we deal with Hispanics and meth it's usually with larger orders and not so much street-type dealing. . . . I don't know if it's any kind of organization that we can break down, but in my experience it's mostly guys that are up there sellin' on the street are just selling to support their habit. And the Hispanics that we come across, it's usually larger amounts of meth. . . .You're talkin' just small gram levels on the street, compared to ounces or more and to pounds.

So hierarchy in the local meth market appears to be the product of a combination of economic factors, ethnicity, and personal association.

Given both this need to recruit local sellers at the retail level and the fact that the wholesalers need to convert large quantities of imported product into small packages for retail sale, the wholesale distribution of methamphetamine in import markets needs to have social patterns and processes that incorporate things like fixed areas of responsibility and levels of authority. As described by a detective from Utah:

> A Mexican national who's kind of a honcho comes to the area. That person comes here with connections already made for the transport of their product to them from Mexico. They've already set up their supply lines before they come here so they know they're going to get the product to get them started. Then they sell that initial product and when they're getting close to getting low they make a phone call or make a correspondence to get that next load coming. Most of the drug sales here are brought by mules that are bringing the drugs to them, with the same mules taking the money back to Mexico. These mules don't normally know or have any kind of connection with the local sellers. They come from the true dealer in Mexico; they're the ones that's sending them, they're the ones paying them. They'll come here and they'll stay for a few days waiting for the local seller here to get enough money to send them back, to make their trip worthwhile. So they're not actually an employee. Seldom do we see salespeople here sending their own people back to Mexico to make pickups because they're so busy here dealing. It does happen but I don't think it happens as often as the drugs are actually being shipped here by that independent party in Mexico.

Thus we have an example of how methamphetamine is distributed from the manufacturer in Mexico through the transporter to the local sales representative of the manufacturer, and how everyone knows what they are supposed to do and how they are supposed to do it.

In Oregon the meth dealer whose family originally came from Mexico before he grew up in California where he worked as a crack dealer on city street corners and then moved to Oregon where he sold methamphetamine, told a similar story.

Crystal [meth] comes straight from the border, all the way from Mexico. . . . They bring pounds and they . . . deliver to other Hispanics, the same people all the time. They break it up and sell it in ounce levels. The people buying ounces and breaking it, they're the ones that's gonna make the money, more than the guy that's selling the whole pound. The people all know each other. Somebody gets busted, another people will come in and do the job. The whites are the one's that's buying it.

As someone who knew the crack business he could see the difference in the meth business in how it was brought to a region for distribution to consumers to be sold through local dealers. His insight reflects what we observed about how the social activity of retail meth distribution is structured.

METHAMPHETAMINE RETAIL SALES AS SOCIAL ACTIVITY

The social structure of retail transactions in methamphetamine markets similarly varies when comparing sales involving local mom-and-pop businesses and sales in markets where the meth is imported. From our respondents we learned that in markets with local labs the cooks sell directly to consumers for personal and immediate use. In import markets there is a more structured hierarchical arrangement with lines of authority and responsibility through which the importer sells larger quantities to a local middle-level distributor who then sells smaller quantities to a local retailer who is known to and trusted by consumers from the local community. The final retail sale invariably involves a seller and buyer who are known to each other (this phenomenon will be discussed in more detail in the next chapter when we talk specifically about social relationships). According to our survey, police respondents said that in 93 percent of the meth market transactions in their area the buyers and sellers know each other.

As noted earlier, on the retail level, mom-and-pop operations produce small quantities of meth and operate like social collectivities or even social clubs. A local cook makes what he or she can and sells (or barters) what he or she can make to family, friends, and acquaintances that may even be waiting around while the meth is being cooked. For example, a police respondent in South Carolina described the local mom-and-pop labs in his area as follows:

> [Compared to a lab described earlier, this] was pretty much the same thing; the individual was just cooking for his friends. It's just interesting because it seems like every lab we run across there is some sort of nexus. There's someone who's either cooking or getting meth from the other labs. We'll have a group of individuals that all they do is shop the pseudoephedrine and then you have a handful of people that are cooking the meth. It's a vast, vast network of individuals. I mean it's shocking to see how much of these people actually know each other. There's a handful that will get some, go to strip clubs, bars in the area, hand it out for sexual favors, things of that nature, we've heard stories of that. It's not like there's an organization that's manufacturing large quantities of meth and packaging it for distribution and just strictly selling it to anybody that wants to buy meth. These people are all networked. They have something in common. They work together; they're family members, they're friends. They all know each other. It's very seldom you'll find someone show up and buy meth that no one knows.

Users and dealers we talked to told similar stories. In a small rural town in Georgia we spoke to a female meth user who bought meth from several different dealers. All of them were people she knew, often well enough that she would place an order and they would deliver the product to her home. And she had known them all for several years. She told us she had no friends when she was straight, so she hung out with the same crowd of meth users. A meth cook from the same area in Georgia described to us how a crowd of users would wait around while he was cooking to get high together when he was done.

A state trooper in Indiana, an area with a large number of local meth labs and little imported methamphetamine, described how the social club environment of the local labs compares to the business model of the Mexican import markets.

> Our experience with the Mexican stuff, we did get some Mexican ice. You know, you could make Mexican ice that's pure garbage. And that's what we were getting. It looked beautiful. It looked like crystal glass.

And it was, I think, 30 percent [pure]. What they're doing is they're adding something to it. The Mexican distribution system is all tied to money. So the quality of the dope really makes no difference to them. Just get it out, and get those bucks back. That's in contrast to our cell structures of six to eight people, who sit there and go, "We want to make the best we possibly can." . . . The meth problem that we have is need driven, and instead of the pyramid system that we're used to, instead of the dope going down and the money going up, with a Mr. or Ms. Big on the top there, instead what you've got is a honeycomb type of thing where you've got five people here and they're learning how to cook it. Then they learn how to cook and all of a sudden somebody comes up with another group. But they're very, very tight little groups.

In this case the local mom-and-pop labs are not just like social clubs, but also like business incubators with people learning to cook and moving on to start their own club.

In areas where meth is sold in import markets the retail sales still take place on a small, personal scale between people who know each other and are comfortable with each other. Most meth users in the United States are white, most are men but lots are women too, and they represent a variety of age groups. In Georgia we spoke with a husband and wife who started using together and eventually began selling small amounts of meth. According to both of them, "he brought it home, he was working concrete" and they both used it out of "boredom, just wanting to have a little bit of fun." The first few years they used a lower quality "peanut butter—bathtub, mom-and-pop stuff" and later they moved on to ice that came from the Mexican importers and they "would buy it and sell it to other people, so we could have ours for free." A meth dealer in Virginia who sold meth for Mexican suppliers told us, "In the meth business, you go to somebody's house and people see you there at times and you get to know them. Everybody gets to know you. You're like birds of a feather."

Especially in areas where Mexican immigration is new to the region, the immigrants who are sent from Mexico to serve (in effect) as regional sales representatives or managers for the illicit Mexican drug manufacturing enterprises cannot easily establish working relations with local consumers. So a common practice is for the "sales manager" who is working for the import enterprise or company to recruit a local sales force with an established customer base and subcontract with those individuals to purchase the company's product and sell it to local customers. The detective from Utah who described the wholesale organization in his area described the local retail organization as follows:

> You have your main honcho [from Mexico] who might have three to five local guys [from Mexico] that the honcho has set up, basically has rented each of them a house or rented them an apartment and basically putting them up. Somebody else of course had rented the apartment in their name, one of the users normally or a white chick that the dealers hooked up with here. They're just trying to protect themselves by having somebody put the apartment in their name, and they'll do the same thing with their vehicles. They'll try to get a vehicle for each of the dealers. Again, it's just a junker that's in somebody else's name so they can go out and conduct their operations. That way the honcho is basically safe if they lose this dealer. The honcho, the main seller, if he loses one of his dealers, there's nothing to bring it back to him. The person is expendable. They get arrested, maybe they get deported, maybe they do some time in jail, cars get taken away, and they're right back at it. So that's kind of a loose organization there. The honcho has four or five guys who are trying to sell ounce quantities of meth. And then those guys have white guys buy the meth from them and they sell it to other white guys or white gals and they just slowly break it down from there to the final user who's buying $20 worth of meth.

A police respondent from a smaller community in Arkansas had a bit more to say about pricing at the various levels:

> For a thousand bucks you can buy a solid ounce of ice [imported from Mexico] in Little Rock and bring it up here and make $1,600 to $1,800. Or if they gram it up, they can make a lot of money. The grams have gone up from $100 to $120 of the ice. An eight ball, you can get an eight ball for three hundred bucks cash. The local stuff's [powder cooked in local labs] usually not out on the market. When it is around it still goes for one hundred a gram or three hundred dollars an eight ball. Eight balls average from $300, $400, $500, to $600. Lately, a lot of people are selling peanuts like it's little rock cocaine,

you buy by the tenth instead of by the gram. I think that's just people stretching it out, making more.

As in any business organization, at each level there are fixed areas of responsibility and authority and there are decisions and actions aimed at maximizing profit. And in this case there are also mechanisms to protect the people at the higher levels from disturbances at the lower levels.

Two native white meth users who became dealers in rural Virginia told us how they were recruited by Mexican nationals who moved to the area to set up a subregional hub for the distribution of meth and to open local markets. In both cases they claimed they never asked or ever learned the names of the people they were buying from or with whom they were associated. And in both cases their stories illustrate the importance of personal relationships for a successful retail meth business, even when the product is imported from Mexico. One man described how after he started using he eventually left a legitimate job to become a meth retailer. As a user he bought from only one guy, but as a dealer he was able to provide meth from a variety of local Mexican wholesale suppliers who got to know him as trustworthy and as someone from whom local users would buy meth. As he explained it:

> I was always straight up with my dealers. That's the way I got started: small amounts, supporting my habit. Then somewhere along the way a friend of mine who was personally selling for the Mexicans ripped me off a couple of times, so I quit messing with him. Next thing I know the Mexicans showed up at my house. And once you start in with the Mexicans, they're in competition too. So once you get in with them, then here comes another one. They got to know me through other people. I've always been pretty straight, even in the drug business. And I had a good reputation with these guys. Guys would come to me and say, "Hey mine's better, I'll let you have it a little cheaper." . . . We [white dealers] are more trustworthy to [the white customers] for a lot of people. Everybody here knows everybody. I got a chosen few customers who I move the product to. The Mexicans are not interested in my [retail] customers. They're just interested in moving their product.

The other Virginia meth dealer noted above described how he was found by a local white woman who had a relationship with a Mexican dealer and was set up in business to sell small quantities to local native white users:

> I guess I have a little bit of an ambitious nature to me. So instead of buying it I decided, you know, I'd buy enough so I could sell a little and support my own habit. I never started dealing to think I'd make money. It just happened eventually. An ex-girlfriend introduced me to my first dealer, a Hispanic dealer. I bought a quarter ounce and started selling it to my friends, a half gram or a gram at a time, just enough to break even and to keep myself high. And I guess eventually I didn't rip off my dealer, I know he made money, so the process got better and maybe the quality of the dope got better. And I graduated on up to maybe an ounce or two at a time through the first Hispanic I was getting from. Then he got busted and I guess, once you're in the drug scene . . . I had another girl introduce me to another Hispanic. And pretty much the same deal. I didn't have any money. He fronted me. All the dope comes from Mexico. You don't ask a lot of questions to these guys. They're already paranoid enough. . . . When my second dealer quit, I got it like he got it. He was a middleman, so when he quit I got a lot better deal because he wasn't pinching out [taking an extra share of the price off the top]. It was a noticeable difference. I got up to a quarter pound and sold that to just two or three people.

He went on to say he could sell more and his dealer wanted him to and he had the customers who would buy from him, but sometimes he was just too high to take care of business.

SOCIAL ACTIVITY IN METH MARKETS

Since methamphetamine markets are social organizations the patterns of behavior among participants are normative and become institutionalized to maximize the ability of market participants to engage in successful social transactions. In other words, because the activity of the people who participate in meth markets is socially organized some of them are able to make meth and get it to people who use it and are able and willing to pay to have it.

In a small town in southeastern Georgia not far from Atlanta we talked with a husband and wife who had been involved with methamphetamine, buying, selling, and using, for a many years. For more than fifteen years the husband had been using and stopping and even spending some time in jail. When his youngest son was born he stopped using, then he started again. They became involved with meth in different ways but they never had trouble getting enough for their own use, and sometimes enough to sell some and have enough left for themselves. We asked them for a typical example of how, when they were selling larger quantities, they would get some product and bring it back home. The story that the husband tells clearly illustrates how his involvement and his decisions and actions in relation to other people with whom he is engaged in what is essentially a business transaction taking place outside of the law is socially organized:

> A lot of the time we were working down at the strip clubs. And a lot of times it was brought up in conversation and other times when we were getting into the bigger amounts you know we would go into Atlanta like up in the Buckhead district or East Lake. Real nice. I mean three, four, five hundred thousand dollar homes. And you're walking in and the guy's got a cooler [laughs] with just Tupperware dishes, just packed [with meth]. And you go and you hang out for a minute and smoke some pot. I guess at the time I thought I was just [laughing again] hangin' out with Scarface and all. But that's just kinda how it was. I mean, it was like livin' in a movie sometimes. I mean parties, and you would get into, "Hey, you and your buddy, we're gonna have a party here next weekend, come by!" And you know, you pull up in an '86 Mercury Cougar and there's Rolls Royces and Bentleys and I'm like not like them. But when you're movin' that kind of weight for some people, they don't care. They're just like, "Come on back!"

Simply looking through the lens of social behavior at his experience of buying methamphetamine from people with money to sell it to people without money is interesting. More interesting is the way that even given their social class distinction and the inevitable societal barriers that consequently separate their lives, their business relationship through their mutual interest in buying, selling, and using methamphetamine follow normative patterns of behavior. Their relationship through their commercial interest is civil and decorous and adheres to institutionalized patterns of behavior organized in a way that allows them to experience a successful transaction that satisfies them both. This raises the question of how social relationships in the methamphetamine industry are formed, maintained, and even what they are like. This is the question that we turn to in the next chapter.

CHAPTER 4

Social Relationships in the
Methamphetamine Industry

PEOPLE NEED TO LEARN how to make methamphet-
amine. It may be easy to learn what chemicals you need and how to
mix them to produce methamphetamine, but knowing how to make
meth safely and how to produce a product that has the desired effect
is something else. The production of methamphetamine is a hazardous
enterprise. Of greatest concern, making methamphetamine involves mixing chemicals that when they are combined in the wrong way or at the
wrong time or when a minor mistake is made in the cooking process
there can be an explosion. Consider the currently popular way to make
small amounts of meth at home or in a car or even while riding a bicycle
that was described in the last chapter, shake-and-bake. First you need
a two-liter bottle and then you need to gather the ingredients, including pseudoephedrine (usually from cold medicines, easily obtained from
smurfers interested in sharing the product with a cook who will make
it for them), lithium metal (you can get this from batteries), and anhydrous ammonia (visit your local farm supply store if you do not have any
around). There are any number of websites and online videos that will
tell you exactly what you need to have and how to mix the ingredients,
as well as the precautions you need to take to avoid being blown up.
Another idea, probably a better one, is to have someone who has experience and knows how to cook meth and knows how to make good meth
teach you what they know.

As is true for any other job-related skill, in the world of making
methamphetamine it helps to have a mentor. For example, when we
were in Georgia we met with the man we mentioned earlier who had
been arrested and jailed for making meth after he had been very seriously
burned in an explosion. Still, he considered himself a good cook who

55

simply had gotten careless. He was good because he had been trained well. Early on his brother-in-law had been teaching him the business and it was not going well. Then a girl he knew introduced him to an older gentleman known for the quality of his work who took him on as a sort of apprentice. He worked with and for him until he was ready to go out on his own. That is, a personal relationship with someone who is a skilled and successful meth cook is a good thing to have if you want to start a successful meth-making business of your own. The man we were talking to told us he blew himself up because he had become overconfident and gave in to too much pressure from his loyal customers to work fast and make lots, so regrettably he ended up trying to cook meth in six bottles at the same time.

A lesson from this man's story from a jail cell in Georgia is that personal relationships matter in methamphetamine markets and in the methamphetamine industry. His experience demonstrates the personal side of how one individual learns to be a meth cook and how that person learns to sell methamphetamine and find and work with his or her customers. In the world of methamphetamine the same is true in how people find work or are recruited into the meth business. During our travels across America we spent some time in Yuma, Arizona. In terms of illicit drugs, one thing that makes Yuma particularly interesting is its location, just about twenty miles from a border crossing into Mexico in San Luis, Arizona.

Beyond the metropolitan areas of Phoenix and Tucson, Yuma is the largest city in Arizona (VisitYuma.com 2013). It was founded in 1871, originally as Arizona City. Today it is the country seat of Yuma County, which also includes the town of San Luis. Its boosters refer to data from the National Climatic Data Center of the National Oceanic and Atmospheric Association when they note, "We're also officially the sunniest [though not the hottest] city in the United States, as well as the driest, least humid and the city with the least frequent days of precipitation" (National Climatic Data Center 2013). The 2010 Census counted 93,064 people living in the city compared to 77,515 in 2000. In the winter months when the weather gets cold in other parts of the country, residents estimate that the local population doubles in size. Being so close to the border with Mexico, it is not surprising that nearly 60 percent of the people living in Yuma are of Hispanic origin.

The two largest legitimate industries in Yuma are agriculture and the military, with Yuma being home to the Marine Corps Air Station Yuma and the U.S. Army Yuma Proving Ground. But given its proximity to the border with Mexico, it is not surprising that another industry that does pretty well in the area is the illicit drug industry, including methamphetamine. During our visit we met with a team of local narcotics police officials and officers. We scheduled an hour for our talk and three hours later we were still talking. They had a lot to tell us about not only local use but also the large-scale movement of illicit drugs from across the border in Mexico into the United States and through the Yuma area for distribution to people all over the country. As one said to us, "Our dope trade within the community, the city, the county, whatever you wanna call it, it's kind of a free for all." Another officer who has been working in methamphetamine enforcement for a long time went on to say, "There's more and more dope coming across the border than there ever has been. It doesn't even make the news now. I mean, you don't even raise an eyebrow on poppin' say twenty-eight keys [kilos] of meth comin' across the border."

After the interview the police we were talking to introduced us to an officer working with the U.S. Border Patrol. He took us in his truck and drove to San Luis to eat tacos and tour the border. He showed us various crossing points and explained how people in Mexico are trained to climb the border fence and where they can find nearby safe houses to stay while they are on their way to their destination elsewhere in the United States. We were there in 2011. A year later, in July 2012, a reporter for the *Arizona Republic* and its online version, azcentral.com, wrote a story under the title "240-Yard Border Tunnel near Yuma Tied to Meth Smuggling." A tunnel for moving methamphetamine from Mexico to the United States had been built just under the buildings where we were eating tacos.

A particularly interesting story we heard in Yuma shows the importance of social relationships for doing business in the methamphetamine industry. One of the police officers told us how a few years earlier people in the area who were meth users had been complaining about the quality of local meth. He said, "But then . . . ice was really starting to become prevalent." The ice or crystal form of methamphetamine was gaining a reputation, deserved or not, as being higher quality meth. The officer continued, "And where was the ice comin' from?" The ice, it turns out, was coming to the area from labs in southwestern California around the San Bernardino area. These labs "actually were not being run by Mexican nationals [people from Mexico]. They [the Mexican nationals] were being coached, basically instructed by Americans who knew how to cook ice. The [Mexican] cartels said, hey, you know what, we're gonna get in on this." This was not surprising, since there was money to be made. The illicit drug cartels from Mexico then started to take over and operate labs in California. There were other groups still operating a few labs, including some biker gangs and a few street gangs, but the Mexican cartels had an advantage in that the labor force working in the labs was largely made up of Mexican nationals or Mexican Americans, giving the cartels a connection with the local workforce that the biker and street gang manufacturers did not have. Some of the workers were members of La Eme (pronounced M-A), a U.S. prison gang composed of Mexican Americans. So the cartels increased their share of the local production industry and were able to get the locally trained workers to work for them. Eventually the cartels from Mexico owned and operated the labs in California and both Mexican Americans, including the La Eme members released from prison, and Mexican nationals worked in those labs.

Social scientists have long recognized that individuals in everyday life relate to one another and that those actions can result in some outcome, whether anticipated or desired or not, when the people involved agree on what the action means and act accordingly. Simply, for people to do and accomplish anything together they have to understand each other. One actor has to understand the words and the actions of the other actor or actors so he or she knows how to respond in an appropriate way that will help them reach a meaningful goal. This is made easier when the people involved know one another.

In the case of an illicit drug industry or market, such as methamphetamine, interactions involving suppliers, distributors, dealers, and consumers or users can involve relationships that are more or less formal, reliable, familiar, open, trustworthy, responsive, sociable, intimate, and so on. In our survey of law enforcement agencies, 94 percent of respondents reported that in their jurisdiction meth buyers repeatedly use the same seller and 93 percent reported that buyers and sellers know each other. In this chapter our attention focuses on various aspects of social relationships in the methamphetamine industry and markets. Given these responses to our survey questions it should not be surprising that what we found are ways that participants in methamphetamine markets maximize the likelihood of achieving the desired outcomes of their actions and interactions by using, if not exploiting, their personal relationships with others.

SOCIAL RELATIONSHIPS AND THE RECRUITMENT AND TRAINING OF METH MARKET WORKERS

For the methamphetamine industry to be able to bring the drug from producers to consumers, a number of relationships have to be established between and among the people involved in the production, distribution, sale, and use of the product. For sales to occur, especially given the need for personal knowledge and interpersonal comfort in meth markets, relationships need to be formed and nurtured among sellers and buyers. For example, a police officer who works narcotics cases in the Yuma, Arizona, area told us: "Here you have to know somebody to really go buy. You don't find a cold buy around here. . . . They may not be blood type relationships, but they have to have some type of relationship." And that relationship needs to involve some measure of trust. A successful meth dealer in rural Virginia told us, "Yeah, I guess I had a pretty good reputation in the meth business because as it was when I got it that's the way I sold. I did not cut it [adulterate it with other substances]. That's what got me into it. It was people. . . . You get to know them and they just spread it around for me."

Getting people who can be trusted and can get along with others is important in the methamphetamine business, so getting the right people to work in sales is particularly important. For the business of meth markets to be accomplished people have to be located and recruited to work for the various enterprises, what might be called companies, that make and sell methamphetamine; they have to be trained; and some standards for labor conditions (for better or worse) have to be established.

In the last chapter we talked about the processes by which cars and trucks and other vehicles are used to transport methamphetamine. In this chapter we talk about how people are recruited to drive these cars and trucks and how their recruitment involves their relationships with other people. Our study was conducted only in the United States so we did not have an opportunity to learn about recruitment of workers in Mexico to work in the superlabs in Mexico. But by talking to people in the United States who are involved in moving the methamphetamine produced in those superlabs to this country we were able to learn about the recruitment of people to transport the meth produced in Mexico to U.S. towns and cities. On the West Coast, where importers of a variety of illicit drugs have been operating for a long time and where Mexican communities have been long established, a drug policy official in Oregon told us how drivers with their families are recruited to bring methamphetamine up the coast to the Pacific Northwest: "Crystal shards of meth are coming up from California in cars with large loads, all customized with either a hydraulic lift on it, or something. . . . These large loads are all driven by Hispanics. And I personally think they're all connected somehow, because every single one of them has their vehicle manufactured in the same way to hide the stuff; almost every one of them. They've also went to great length to conceal what they were doing. For instance, they would bring their girlfriend and her kids." The advantage of using cars, according to the Oregon respondent, is that "trucks [commercial vehicles] take a lot of coordination. You gotta have contacts." In Georgia, a hub for the distribution of methamphetamine on the East Coast though an area less heavily settled by immigrants from Mexico, a respondent who worked on a local drug crime interagency law enforcement team told us that truck drivers hauling other loads are recruited to move shipments of drugs as they are transferred from one distribution point to another. When they stop at a rest area they are asked if they would take some amount of money to leave the truck for an hour or so while something is placed in it, drive to a designated location, and leave the truck again for an hour or so. Then all they have to do is drive away with the extra cash in their pocket.

Aside from recruiting workers to transport methamphetamine to an area, people in the area also have to be recruited to sell meth in the local retail markets. Sometimes people in the business are recruited through their friends or families, as was the case described by a woman who was a user and dealer in Staunton, a rural town in Virginia:

> I was born into it. My mother was a drug dealer. My whole family was into drugs. My mom was a meth addict. I first did methamphetamine when I was nine years old. I then became addicted. I sold drugs all my teenage years to take care of my mother 'cause my

mother was an addict. Instead of her making her money she did her product. . . . When I was fourteen I got my own dealer and started selling it myself. A couple of friends introduced me to a couple of people who dealt drugs, and I ended up becoming a runner [someone who moves illicit drugs from one place or person to another, such as from a wholesale distributor to a retail seller or a seller to a buyer]. I sold their dope, I made their money, and I made mine. Plus I had my product to smoke. I sold anywhere from five to ten eight balls a day. I didn't sell to just anybody. And I was using an eight ball myself every day. I was making loads of money, and just blowin' it.

Sometimes a user gets so caught up in use that little else matters. In rural Virginia, for example, another woman who was using meth heavily allowed her dealer to reach her children and recruit them for both his customer base and as potential business associates. She told us: "My daughter was thirteen when I was using. She knew. She tried it, and I knew she did. One of my dealer's friends turned her on to it. . . . The dealers, that's how they do it. They sneak behind your back and get to your kids. You're so high you don't do the right things to try to protect them." She went on to say that "when you get high enough you're really no good to nobody."

It is not uncommon for sex and sexual relations to play a part in social interactions or relationships, so naturally sex and sexual relations have a role in the distribution of methamphetamine, notably in local retail markets. Typically this involves meth dealers and producers leveraging their supply of the drug to extract sexual and other favors from drug users. However, we found that the role of sex in social interaction in meth markets takes different forms in different market contexts. In terms of participants interacting at the retail level in a local market where meth is produced in local mom-and-pop labs, one police respondent in Ohio described trading meth for sex and other favors: "Well, typically, what you'll find—I guess you would call it prostitution; what they call them on the street are 'jar-jumpers.' And they're women usually with a kid or two that will hook up with a meth cook and their sole reason for hooking up with the meth cook is their meth supply. And they will run errands and stuff for the meth cook and hide him out in their homes and that kind of stuff but they are actually paid, you know, services for sex. I mean the only reason why they're there is protection and sex." More than 71 percent of our survey respondents reported prostitution (broadly defined) to be common among methamphetamine users and dealers.

Sexual relations also have a place in areas where imported methamphetamine has supplanted local production. In these areas the sexual dynamics of relationships in meth markets can more clearly be seen in terms of recruitment. For example, sexual relationships serve to provide an important connection between wholesalers who are from outside of the local area and not known to local people and the users and dealers who know and trust each other and personally participate in the local retail markets. When asked about how methamphetamine moves from wholesale to retail markets, two police officers from Virginia, an area where most of the methamphetamine is imported from Mexico, described the importance of sexual relationships in helping wholesalers from outside of the area identify and establish relationships with local users who can work for them as retailers. One said, "A lot of times the Hispanics will have girlfriends who do all of the dealing for them. That's probably typical. . . . The first thing they want to do is get around an American woman and get in the system—it happens all the time." So in their experience and as described by a family service provider from the area, women form personal relationships with Mexican men in the drug trade and then introduce them to native white men they know who are users, need money, and are good recruits to become sellers. However it is used and whoever uses it, sex is an important part of the interactions and personal relationships among methamphetamine producers, dealers, and users at all levels and in all types of markets.

A man we wrote about earlier who sold drugs in a rural community in Virginia explained how he got into the meth dealing business. Earlier our focus was on how he was recruited. Here our focus is on the importance of personal relationships and trust in the way he was able to get established in the business. He started as a user and then people who knew him to be trustworthy and knew he used meth himself then trusted him to be fair and to get good product for them. Eventually he became a full-time meth dealer when he was recruited to open an outlet for distributors who had come to the area from Mexico to sell imported crystal. He told us:

At one time I was just dealing with this one guy. I was just buying from him. I wasn't dealing at that point. I was living from payday to payday just to get some more. So I think, well, I could quit my job and do like all the rest of them [guys]. They had never worked and it was just the way it worked. So I met some other people and they let me just take some [meth] and pay them for it next week, maybe half an ounce or something. That's how I got started into dealing. I was getting enough to support my habit. . . . It was people I met along the way. Once you get into methamphetamine, it's best that you start dealing. I mean, I was always straight up with these guys, you know. They would think nothing about giving me methamphetamine and I tell him I'll pay him next week. And that's the way I got started in small amounts, you know, supporting my habit. And then somewhere along the way, a friend of mine introduced me to a Mexican [distributor] and he ripped me off a couple of times, so I just quit dealing. The next thing I know, another Mexican showed up at my house. He wanted me to start dealing for him. Once you get in with them, then here comes another one to get to know you. They have to trust you and you have to trust them.

Another meth dealer from that same area described how he started working as a local dealer for a Mexican distributor that he met through his girlfriend.

An ex-girlfriend introduced me to my first dealer, a Hispanic dealer. . . . Her friend, a girl, she was dating one of the Hispanics, and they all—about five of them—lived in a trailer. And I was naïve at that point; I didn't know what they were doing. I just knew that they had meth and I wanted to use meth. So I had no idea that they had the capacity that I could eventually get a hold of quantity other than just—so I just bought from them for the longest time. You don't just go in and say, "Hey, I know you got dope, do you mind? I can probably move a lot of dope for you"—you know, not like that because that will come through a lot of red flags and you never know. . . . [Eventually] I started with like a quarter ounce and selling it to my friends, half a gram or a gram at that time and basically just breaking even, having enough money to go back and get another quarter of an ounce and had kept myself high for a period while I had something. . . . I guess that once you're in the drug scene and the drug culture, if you let it suck you in, everybody that you associate with is a user.

In both of these cases the local dealer started as a user and got involved in the methamphetamine business through personal relationships. In both cases the situation involved local users getting to know people working for the conglomerates in Mexico. A researcher in Georgia who studies local methamphetamine markets told us that "in talking to people about how they get people interested in the product, for example, a Mexican person at the mid-level will have runners at the retail level who will typically be white."

Social interaction and personal relationships are also important for manufacturing methamphetamine at the local level. Making methamphetamine does not require a graduate degree in chemistry, but, as noted earlier, it is something you have to learn to do. Often in the local mom-and-pop lab businesses training can be accomplished through a sort of mentorship program where a cook trains someone to help him or her as an apprentice until that person can have their own business. The meth cook from Georgia discussed in the introduction to this chapter described how he learned the trade after his own drug use had cost him his family and he was not able to find a job. His experience also illustrates how the trainee while learning is also helping the trainer in his or her business: "[I was taught] by just this old guy. Actually, my brother-in-law, he tried to show me. But I knew just from doing it the old way that he didn't know what he was doing. It didn't seem right. So I experimented by myself. It really wasn't that bad, but then this guy come along that this girl that I knew, she knew him. And she said, 'Why don't you let him show you how to do it. He makes it a lot better.' So I did, and then basically from then on I just cooked for him. He never charged me or nothing to show me how to do it." At his peak this trainee became good enough that by his own account he could "make an eight ball in an hour."

Sometimes the local cook will provide training to the people who are in his or her social circle as user customers. During a telephone interview that took place with a Google map of the respondent's area in front of him and the site of a meth lab seizure highlighted, a police respondent in Minnesota described a local lab in his area where this was the case:

"Yes, there was an active cook in that lab. We actually hit that one while they were cooking, arrested five people on that one; white males and females. I think it was anhydrous. This was ounce level. They were going to keep it all within the five of them. One of the women there was a cook that was actually teaching the others to cook, and we had busted her in a nearby city two years earlier, about fourteen miles north of us. And that was some amazing fluff meth; very light, light, airy powder. I've never seen stuff like it before. Originally she was taught by bikers." For meth users, as for users of any substance, quality has a subjective element. But producing it a certain way takes a level of skill. In this case the respondent apparently was impressed by the lightness of the product and the skill it took to make it. Similarly, a narcotics detective in Ohio told us about an arrest his department made of a man who claimed to have introduced meth to his area by training other people to make it:

> It was a guy and his girlfriend. They got into a fight. She called us, we showed up. We ended up arresting him. He said he was doing scientific experiments. Of course, you know, that was not true. He ended up going to prison, he gets out and we ended up getting him again on another meth lab. While I talked to him about all this stuff and word on the street, through interviews with him, he basically spelled out that he was the one that actually introduced this meth in this area. He started teaching people how to do it and then once he went to prison the first time, that's when it kind of blew up that all these other cooks started their enterprise. They taught people and then they taught people and the next thing you know we have a whole county full of meth cooks.

In this way the cooks in the local labs can pass on their knowledge for making meth to the people who will become the meth cooks of the future.

Learning to cook meth and becoming known as a good cook can be a source of status in a community of users. A drug treatment provider in a city in Oregon explained to us how and why this can be a problem:

> Our meth population, we've got a couple of different kinds. We got the ones that just never got anything. They're kind of the bottom dweller. A part of that population lives from one little quarter of

gram bag to the next. And then you got the ones that are engaged in some low-level street dealing, and then you've got the guys who do the manufacturing, and they've got a little bit of a status thing going. Unfortunately, they create a bit of a problem for us in treatment because the younger ones want to gravitate towards them. They want to learn, they want to try to turn treatment into a jailhouse environment where they can learn their cooking trade kind of thing.

The problem, he pointed out, is that this makes it harder "to work with them to develop job skills and responsibility and accountability and consistency."

SOCIAL RELATIONSHIPS AND MARKETING METHAMPHETAMINE

In the methamphetamine industry social relationships are also important for opening new markets and building new clientele. People matter. Mindful that methamphetamine and its markets are illegal, unlike legitimate businesses it is not easy to conduct public opinion surveys or marketing research studies to determine the viability of a new market. Some regions and several big cities known for their drug-using populations have not been easy to open to the methamphetamine industry. There may be lots of heroin or cocaine users in a city, but that does not necessarily mean that the same city will be a good market for methamphetamine sales. For example, in a town in Illinois a narcotics detective described with some surprise how difficult it was to introduce meth in his area:

There's so much cocaine, crack, heroin, marijuana in this area. Meth is like the new drug on the block and we haven't been encountering that many labs making meth. There have been a few but not that many, which is just the opposite of what's going on in the rest of the state. You go to the southern part of the state or other areas, meth is probably their biggest problem. Like 80, 90 percent of their problem is methamphetamine. Here, it seems like the last four or five meth cases that we have, we've been picking off the multipound quantities coming in from the Southwest border to Illinois. So it appears that the Mexican cartel is trying to open up a market for meth in the area and it seems like they really don't have that great of a customer base and that they're trying to build a customer base.

In this case the detective was describing the difficulty in general of opening a new drug market.

In a city in the Middle Atlantic region with an established heroin- and cocaine-using population, meth dealers to their surprise and dismay have not been able to open the market. In this case there was a specific incident that clearly demonstrated the problem. The incident started as an undercover, multistate operation to investigate a drug ring distributing cocaine to the city and in the end became a methamphetamine case. Detectives operating undercover as drug dealers from their city were trying to purchase cocaine from the distributors working in another state and were offered methamphetamine on consignment to be used to open meth markets in their city. As described by a team of detectives who work undercover drug cases for the city police department and were involved with this case: "It started as a smaller case and it just got bigger and bigger. Started and done in three weeks. We went to [a southern state], then we went to [a southern city], then we came back in, then we went back to [the southern state]. They fronted us six pounds [of meth], so eventually you got to pay the money. And we're not gonna pay out hundreds of thousands of dollars to them to continue a case, so you have to move quickly to close that thing down." The detectives regularly work cases where they work their way into a cocaine distributing organization and are eventually fronted quantities of the drug, but never had they been fronted so much cocaine, particularly in such a brief span of time. "We get fronted cocaine all the time," one told us. In this case they had the money to pay for a kilo of cocaine, and paid the dealer for that. So they "passed the test." They were considered legitimate. Then they were given methamphetamine worth $150,000 to $200,000 wholesale without having to show the money and by people who only had their cell phone number, license plate tag number, and a reference from another drug dealer. The reference from the other dealer was important. As one of the detectives told us:

> The suppliers want a new market. They're dying for a new market, and they really love the idea of opening an East Coast meth customer [base]. So we went to talk about coke originally, and they offered meth. The guy who had been talking to them, the broker guy we had been working with [who we had arrested] had already

gotten marijuana from them, and they wanted to give him meth. He wasn't sure he could get rid of it, and that's where we came in. We said, oh yeah, you can get rid of it. Now, the guy we were working with was trying to find a way to get rid of it and they trusted him.

Since there are so many known cocaine and heroin users in the target city, and since all of these drugs are in fact illegal, the out-of-state drug dealer with whom they were negotiating probably had not conducted any focus groups or marketing surveys. But he had good reason to believe that it should be possible to introduce methamphetamine to the city so he trusted people he knew because as far as he knew (not knowing that they were really undercover law enforcement officers) he had already done business with them. Since the case was actually a criminal investigation and not a business transaction, that turned out to be a bad idea. The detectives who received the meth never had any intention of trying to open meth markets back home. And to this day, with few exceptions, methamphetamine markets have not made significant inroads into the illicit drug user community of that city.

Just because a particular product is successfully bought and sold in one place does not mean that it will be easy or even possible to open a market for that product in another place. And just because one product is known to be successfully bought and sold in a particular place does not mean that it will be possible to open a market in that place for a product that is considered comparable to the one that is already successfully being marketed. Opening a new market for a new product is not easy. For decades national statistics have shown higher levels of methamphetamine use in areas in the western part of the country, but not much if any in the East. Also, different from many other illicit drugs, meth has always had a following in rural communities, maybe even more than in urban areas. So it is not surprising that drug dealers trying to open methamphetamine markets in cities and towns with large populations of users of other drugs, such as heroin or cocaine, are not finding success. The people who use and are attracted to methamphetamine are not necessarily the same people who use and are attracted to cocaine, heroin, or other illicit drugs. Unfortunately for the entrepreneurs, you have to understand that personal user dynamic and you have to be careful who you trust.

THE IMPORTANCE OF
PERSONAL RELATIONSHIPS IN
METHAMPHETAMINE MARKETS

As noted, studies of heroin and cocaine markets, including crack cocaine markets, have focused on street sales. In the case of crack, for example, findings from the scholarly research as well as the news reports of journalists and the fictionalized stories of crime novels and television series have highlighted transactions on street corners, often involving strangers. Methamphetamine markets are different in that personal relationships are a critical element of market transactions. Meth is rarely if ever sold to strangers. In addition to the finding that 93 percent of our survey respondents reported that meth buyers and sellers in their area know each other, during all of our telephone interviews and site visits we asked our respondents: "If I came to your area and wanted to buy meth, where would I go?" Consistently they came up with some variant of the following: "You can't. You have to know someone." In one city in the Southwest we asked a taxicab driver where we could buy meth, assuming taxicab drivers meet a lot of people and know a lot of things. Once we convinced him that we were legitimate researchers and neither undercover detectives nor meth dealers, he told us that there was no way we would be able to buy meth in his city without someone to vouch for us. In Portland, Oregon, a meth dealer we were interviewing told us we could not get it ourselves, but if we were to give him our money he could get it for us.

During our telephone interview with a narcotics detective in a small town in New Mexico he pointed to places on the Google map we were showing him through his computer where we might go to buy various drugs. When we asked specifically about meth he told us that before we could buy any we would have to be known by the seller: "They [the meth dealers] have to know you before they'll start selling to you. You have to get connected with them and then they have to take some time. And once they get to know you, they'll sell to you on a regular basis almost as much as you want." A native white woman in Georgia who had been a meth user for a long time told us that she and her husband got started buying powder from a white guy they knew who was making it himself. Later when they moved on to ice they got it from the same guy, but he got it from "the Mexicans." The seller was "just somebody I knew who was able to get it for us, so he did."

As described earlier, the problem of methamphetamine sales having to take place between people who are comfortable interacting with one another takes on an interesting dimension, particularly in communities where the methamphetamine is imported from Mexico and the Mexican population in the area has only recently arrived. When asked about who his customers would buy from, a meth dealer in Virginia told us: "I'm sure it doesn't have to be a white person, but from my experience they prefer to use a white person. Maybe it's just that's their way of being cautious or, I mean, trying to protect themselves. I think the biggest reason is they try to find one person they can trust." The point is that trust is important for business transactions to be possible. Interestingly, this works both ways. A detective in Georgia outside of Atlanta told us that meth distributors moving to his area from Mexico prefer to work with other Hispanics: "Because the Mexican cartels control most of the drug trade, most of the major distribution groups, most of the major importers and exporters, there is a Hispanic element to it. [And] they don't trust Caucasians or whites. They trust the people that they deal with on a daily basis, which is the Hispanic community." It is also important to note that, as he said, "For the most part the Hispanic population moving in here is not involved in the drug trade."

Not having a contact does not mean it will never be possible to get methamphetamine. The new user just has to take time and make the effort to get to know someone who knows someone who can serve as a reference. For example, a detective in a small town in Oklahoma told us, "If he [the meth dealer] doesn't know you, he's not going to sell to you. Now if somebody introduces you into it then you might be able to buy some there." The detective from New Mexico who told us about the need to be known by the seller provided an example of making contacts. There is a military base near his jurisdiction and we asked about how people stationed there would get meth if they were interested. They are not part of the local community and not known to local people, but they do spend a good deal of time in the area. He told us that if they did not have methamphetamine delivered directly to the base then they could start spending time in local bars where meth users and dealers hung out until people got to know them and would be comfortable enough to sell to them.

For people new to a community the local bars seem to be a good way to get to know and be known by people involved in selling, buying, and using meth and to establish the personal relationship necessary to buy meth. From the dealer perspective, a long-time meth dealer from Oregon told us, "You have to know people, you have to be around." When we met him he was working with the local police and told us how he had to convince them to allow him to continue to associate with his old user and dealer friends and acquaintances so he could be useful to the police as a confidential informant. He said, "Like I told them [the police], if I have to work with them I have to be around them [dealers], or else there ain't gonna be no people for me to work with." When we asked him where we would go in the area to buy meth he smiled and told us, "You go to one of the bars, Mexican bars, right there. But they have to see you with one of us. 'He's with him, no sweat.' People that go downtown and try to buy dope alone, that's where you get bad stuff, stepped on." And we heard a similar perspective from a woman in Oregon who was a meth user and the mother of three other meth users. When asked she told us, "Once you get somebody to trust you. Luckily for me I was able to do that. I'm easy to talk to, and they open up a lot."

A detective from a town in Louisiana told us, "We're still somewhat of a rural area so most of these people grow up and they know each other around here quite a bit. We have certain bars and stuff that I guess the [people from the same] subculture will hang out at and meet each other, go through those meetings, so quite a few of them do know each other." Similarly, a detective from a small town in Nebraska told us how this can work even in an import market. He described how Mexican importers new to his area worked through established native white bikers in local biker bars to find customers for meth: "They're selling mostly to the biker bars, to the Caucasians. They [the bikers] know who they can sell to. They make contacts mostly in some of the smaller communities and they have a pretty good intelligence system, too. They have friends that they know that know friends in certain areas and build up their contacts."

Besides bikers there are other subcultures of methamphetamine users and being part of one of those subcultures opens up possibilities for the social interaction and personal relationships necessary to buy and sell methamphetamine. One such subculture of methamphetamine users is found in a number of urban communities among men who have sex with men. According to several accounts men who participate in this subculture use methamphetamine on weekends to enhance their sexual experience and, according to what our various respondents told us, do not use it during the week when they have other responsibilities, such as work. A researcher in Georgia told us: "When you talk about meth in Georgia, you got to make sure you recognize that there are varied populations that use the drug dependent upon where geographically they're located in the state. . . . Individuals who are using meth in the city are much more likely to be gay men and younger users. . . . Crystal got introduced through drug dealers who really marketed to the party, club crowd. . . . There is a population in the city of MSMs [men who have sex with men] who are just recreational users."

Similarly, when we first sat down with a detective from a drug unit in Seattle, Washington, and told him we wanted to ask questions about methamphetamine, he said, "Has anybody talked to you about the homosexual perspective on methamphetamine here?" He continued:

> Oh my gosh, it's infested in the homosexual community. Horribly. And it's also directly associated with HIV and the other STDs. . . . These are highly functional people. They're up for two or three days. . . . And it's very underground. Lots of ads on Craigslist and stuff like that. . . . These are people who for the rest of the week, they're functioning. They're holding jobs. [They're not like the meth users who] can't get across the street by themselves. . . . But [they] will end up like that too. There are a lot of people [in the gay meth using community] who have already crashed.

In addition, a detective in Nevada told us that for gay men in Reno methamphetamine is "a party drug only on the weekend." So an interesting observation here is that, as the researcher from Georgia said, "Not everybody who uses this drug [methamphetamine] gets addicted to it." Of course he is a social scientist, not a natural scientist, so his conclusion about addiction is based on observations of behavior and not necessarily on findings from clinical or biological studies.

Subcultures of methamphetamine users, such as the community of users who are urban men who have sex with men, apparently are not as well understood by those who make and enforce policy as are the wider and more traditional markets of users. A state trooper from rural Illinois who attended a meeting in Chicago described his experience as follows:

> It blew my mind. They had a meth problem, but it wasn't our meth problem . . . First of all, the demographics were so different. It's all gay. All gay! I mean the whole area. I went up there and I'm looking around, I go, "Well this isn't your standard southern Illinois crowd." The terrible concern about it was that they had, in addition to the problem we've got, they've got the problem with HIV. And what they were getting into—this one gentleman he lost his partner, obviously who he was very much connected to, because his partner went to what they call the Twilight Zone, which is a bathhouse area that they allow them to have sex indiscriminately, like all day and all night. And he may have had twelve different partners. And they rode bareback. Which I didn't know what that was, but I learned that it wasn't isolated. . . . Most police officers don't get to see that there are so many different consequences.

He concluded, "It's a whole different ball game."

Another subculture of methamphetamine users that receives limited attention is Native Americans living on reservations. Our respondents in local police departments frequently expressed concern about drug trafficking activities on reservations, but they found that even when they could work with tribal police it was difficult for them to work with tribal governments. Tribal governments were outside the scope of this study, so our knowledge of methamphetamine use in Native American communities is limited to what we were told by people who themselves do not have access to knowledge about methamphetamine on tribal lands. Given that limitation, government officials in Washington State described their perceptions of the methamphetamine industry on tribal lands in the areas near their state. They told us: "The reservations, they have a lot of problems. We work with them, with the tribal police. They're at the whim of the tribal council. And there's a lot of turnover with tribal chiefs. They acknowledge the problem, but they don't know what to do about it. . . . I think they're heavily infiltrated by the Mexican DTOs [drug trafficking organizations]. And they marry into families. They really don't have a lot of meth labs on the reservation. It's all coming from Mexico." So while representatives of local governments and law enforcement have some ideas and opinions about methamphetamine use and distribution among Native Americans, they do not really know and can only tell us what they think is happening. Nonetheless, from the little they do know and are able to share with us it appears that there is overlap between subcultures of methamphetamine users and the larger methamphetamine industry in tribal communities.

SOCIAL RELATIONSHIPS IN METH MARKETS

In the world of legitimate business people are routinely engaged in social interactions involving commercial transactions. And for the most part these interactions involve people who do not know each other or at least do not know one another in a personal way. If you shop often enough in a supermarket you may recognize a clerk at the bakery or the deli counter and you may say hello when you make a purchase, but the people at the counter are not likely to be your friends and you probably do not even know their names. When you check out at the register, if you go to a supermarket that still has cash registers and live cashiers, you may acknowledge the person ringing up your items and taking your money and may even know enough about them to ask a more personal question, like how is your son doing in school (though it is doubtful you can name the son or know what school he is attending). If you see these people on the street you might smile hello, but these are not the same people you would invite to your home or would meet for dinner or a movie. Commercial exchanges in the world of legitimate business may be social interactions but almost invariably they do not involve people who share a close personal relationship. They are social interactions between strangers or at best between distant acquaintances.

The buying and selling of illicit drugs on street corners in urban areas around the country similarly involves commercial exchanges between people in the course of a social interaction. Drugs such as heroin or crack cocaine or, at some time in history, marijuana that are bought by consumers from sellers who operate from the front of a building or the hood of a car are not the stuff of close personal relationships. The buyer and seller might be complete strangers who have never met before, or the buyer might be a regular customer who comes back to the same seller on a regular basis. In the latter case they probably know one another but also probably do not socialize outside of the commercial transaction.

The buying and selling of methamphetamine is different. It requires trustworthy social relationships. For example, earlier in this chapter we wrote about something we heard from a detective in rural Nebraska. He told us over the telephone about the way that methamphetamine was sold in his community from white sellers to white users through local biker bars, and how when importers from Mexico came to the area with their product they established relationships with an established local Mexican population working in legitimate industries to reach the local customer base.

The detective who told us this story was from a small city in Nebraska, Holdrege. In the south-central part of the state and about fifteen miles south of Interstate 80, Holdrege is not far from the Kansas state line and near the geographical center of the United States. According to its website (City of Holdrege, Nebraska 2013), the city was originally settled in the 1880s by immigrants primarily from Sweden. There are a number of active legitimate industries in the city and in the area, and from all accounts it sounds like overall it is a good place to live. But every town and city has things going on around the edges that can disrupt the lives of the majority of people living there who are trying to lead respectable and respectful lives. Apparently one of those things found on the fringe of the area around Holdrege is methamphetamine.

The 2010 Census found that the population of the city of Holdrege was 4,595 people, about half male and half female. According to a page of its website, within fifteen miles of the city there are 11,302 white people, 15 black people, and 515 people of Hispanic origin. But going out fifty miles, there are 116,716 white people, 1,418 black people, and 13,684 people of Hispanic origin. This is interesting in the context of what the detective we spoke with told us, particularly as it relates to the question of the importance of personal relationships and the local methamphetamine markets. At one point in our conversation he noted, "We have Mexicans who have moved up here within the last fifteen, twenty years. They work in meat packing, agriculture, feed and feedlots, and things like that." There is a relatively large population of people of Hispanic origin in the area working in legitimate industries. Arguably having this population in the area was useful to the Mexican cartels when they began moving methamphetamine to the local markets. It allowed them to blend into the local community and not be seen as outsiders so they could establish working relationships with the right people to enhance their opportunities for commercial success.

During our interview with the detective we learned how methamphetamine markets in the area operated outside of the reputable and legitimate parts of the local community. For sales directly to consumers of methamphetamine, most of whom are white, local biker gangs that sell methamphetamine work through local bars they operate. So in those bars the sellers and the buyers of meth were mostly white people and for the most part they knew one another. A problem for the importers coming from Mexico was to be able to reach customers who preferred to buy from people they knew and trusted. So for the importers to establish successful methamphetamine businesses in the area they needed to work through relationships they established with local people of Hispanic origin who already lived and worked in the area. According to what we were told, ultimately they were able to sell to local methamphetamine users, again most of whom were white, through the relationships that indigenous local Hispanic people had with local white people.

In this chapter we described the social interaction and social relationships of people who participate in meth markets and the methamphetamine industry in America. Specifically we described how people involved in the manufacture, distribution, and sales of methamphetamine relate to each and the importance of those relationships for the successful transfer of methamphetamine from sellers to buyers. In this chapter we also begin to see evidence of the importance of culture for a successful methamphetamine market, so in the next chapter we turn our attention to the cultural aspects of methamphetamine markets and the methamphetamine industry.

CHAPTER 5

The Culture of the Methamphetamine Industry

WE LIVE IN A WORLD that is made up of stuff. The world is filled with all those things we can see or smell or hear or taste or touch that we use to do the things we do. In your home, for example, you have something called a chair you can sit on and something called a bed on which you can lie down. If you live in a modern society, in order to communicate with other people you probably have a device you and the people you know call a cell phone or maybe a smartphone that allows you to talk to them when you are not together or to send them electronic mail or text messages. The stuff also includes the words and actions you use to communicate, maybe to describe or explain something. The point is that all this stuff has a shared meaning for the people who use it and the people around them who share the world they live in. In that way they can be part of a group or collective of people that shares the same time and space and has the ability to collaborate or even cooperate to accomplish things, or at least work around each other. Every society and every subgroup of people has their stuff. This is also true for the subgroup of people who participate in the methamphetamine industry.

Among the stuff shared by the people who participate in the methamphetamine industry is the methamphetamine product itself. People who make or sell or use methamphetamine share a common meaning for methamphetamine and how to characterize it. As we have seen in earlier chapters, it can be paste or powder or even look like ice crystals. It can be determined to be good in terms of its ability to make people feel its effects, and sometimes not so good. The people who make or sell or use it all know these things about the stuff called methamphetamine and to some extent they all can agree or at least agree to disagree about the authenticity and quality of the meth they are looking at or tasting or smelling or smoking or injecting.

In 2005 Oregon was the first state in the United States to pass a law (HB 2485) that restricted access to medicinal products that contained pseudoephedrine, requiring that all such products be sold to consumers only when they are prescribed by a doctor. That is, the cook who needed pseudoephedrine to make methamphetamine and the smurfers who would normally be supplying him or her with a sufficient supply of cold tablets all had a problem. From what we heard during our travels and read in local newspapers around the country, Oregon became the benchmark for narcotics police in other states who watched as the local labs making meth in Oregon all went out of business. The closing of the labs may have impacted the supply of meth but it did not diminish the demand for it. The Oregon state line is crossed by I-5, the interstate highway traveling the distance directly from the Mexican border all the way to and through the Oregon border, and it is no surprise that the closing of local labs in Oregon had the unintended consequence of expanding the market for imported methamphetamine from Mexico. This is not to minimize the significance of essentially eliminating a local industry and the local manufacture of a product recognized to be harmful to the health and well-being of people and communities. Nor is it to minimize how important it was to effectively shut down an industry that produced waste known to be immensely harmful to natural resources and the local environment and to the people who had to live with and clean it up. But it does mean that methamphetamine distribution and use in Oregon did not go away.

Located on the interstate highway and at the confluence of the Willamette and Columbia Rivers, Portland is the by far the largest city in Oregon, with 587,865 people, according to the 2010 Census. Seventy-two percent are white, 6 percent are black, and just over 9 percent are of Hispanic origin with the remainder being mostly Asian (7 percent) or of more than one race (5 percent). Most of them are hardworking decent people. Nonetheless, there is a community of people in the Portland area who are involved with methamphetamine, though obviously today they are more likely to be buying or using and not making meth. While we were there we met with the young Hispanic man we talked about earlier who grew up in Los Angeles, where he sold crack before moving to Portland, where he sold methamphetamine until he was arrested. Here his story tells us a little about how the methamphetamine product being sold to consumers in the Portland area changed, today being primarily the ice that is coming up from Mexico.

We met this methamphetamine dealer through the local police. At the time we talked he told us that he was effectively retired from the illicit drug business, trying to find legitimate work to support himself and the four children from different wives who were all in his care. He told us about his involvement as a young gangbanger in the crack cocaine markets in Los Angeles and how he saw and pursued the opportunity to advance his career as an illicit drug dealer in the expanding market for ice in Portland.

Whereas the methamphetamine that is imported from Mexico or produced in superlabs run by the Mexican cartels and is often called ice looks like crystal shards, methamphetamine made in local labs typically looks like powder or paste. There are processes that cooks can use to give the local stuff the appearance of ice, but arguably it is still not the same. People engaged in the manufacture, distribution, or use of meth may have their favorites, but most would agree that ice tends to be more pure than powder or paste. A detective we spoke to by telephone in Walla Walla, Washington, told us that in his area the local cooks are making powder but try to make it into crystal. In his opinion, "They're doing their best to make it into crystal but the purities are real low."

According to the crack dealer from Los Angeles who became an ice dealer in Portland, "Crystal never gets stepped on [diluted with other substances]. Not [when it comes] from over there [Mexico]. It always comes like it is." We asked about the quality, and how willing buyers were to accept that it was high quality. While most dealers who bought from him in Portland believed in the high quality of the product from Mexico, they needed confirmation. "They always test it," he told us. "People buying a couple of ounces at a time, they have to test it. They want to see what it is. [If it's high quality] they can step on it themselves [when they sell it]. They want to leave it like at the 90 or 80 percent, so they can make more money." The point is that they all have to know and agree upon the quality of what they are getting and what they can do with it to be able to sell it. With the crystal from Mexico at such high levels of purity, the local sellers do cut it for sale to their own customers. As the former dealer we were talking to told us, "With crystal, that's what a lot of people does. You can step on it and it's still good."

Broadly, the stuff of our common experience is the substance of society. Social scientists including sociologists and anthropologists call this culture. In the mid-twentieth century the social philosopher Alfred Schutz wrote about the world of cultural objects and social institutions into which we are born and how together they give us our bearing in a world we share with other people. We share with others common meanings assigned to the stuff that makes up the substance of our social experience. Then we as members of a social community are able to live in a world that is both private and public at the same time. In an illicit drug industry and its markets the culture would include patterns of behavior, artifacts, symbols, standards, morals, values, and technology. These are used by participants to understand one another and to know what they have to do to successfully move an illicit product from production through distribution to consumption. Through our survey of police offices, telephone conversations with narcotics detectives, and visits to people who devote at least part of their lives to methamphetamine we observed some cultural elements that were similar and others that varied in different types of methamphetamine markets across and within different parts of the country.

METHAMPHETAMINE AS A PRODUCT

Methamphetamine itself as a product is an artifact of the methamphetamine industry. This not only refers to the quality of the substance but also to things such as the language and measures used to package and distribute the product. Some of it is borrowed from other illicit drug markets, such as weights. Like other drugs, methamphetamine is sold in common weights and measures such as ounces or grams. For example, a drug enforcement official in Hawaii told us, "Powder cocaine is about $200 a gram and crack is about $75 to $150, it depends. Meth is more expensive, about $300 a gram." Methamphetamine, also like other illicit drugs, is sold in quantities exclusively used in illicit drug industries, such as eight balls. A narcotics detective in Texas was asked about the units in which meth is sold in his area. He said, "Just like crack cocaine, in quarter grams, you know, grams, what they call eight ball which is an eighth, or a sixteenth of an ounce, or even an ounce." Of course, as explained to us by a detective in Washington, the price for an eight ball will vary depending on the source and quality of the product: "When I started, for an eight ball we were paying $80 to $90 for the mom-and-pop stuff. When we first got introduced to crystal [from Mexico], it was $120 for an eight ball. We're paying $225 to $350 for an eight ball of crystal, the good glass stuff, right now."

As is true of any product, including illegal drugs, not all methamphetamine is alike. There is variation in quality, appearance, and even taste. Pharmaceutically d-methamphetamine is different from dl-methamphetamine, but the chemistry does not mean much or matter much to the typical meth user. More important is that d-meth (the contemporary product made using pseudoephedrine methods) compared to dl-meth (made with older methods favored by biker cooks in the early days of methamphetamine in the United States) gives them more of the effects they like with less bothersome side effects. In the late twentieth and early twenty-first centuries when meth cooks in rural communities made d-meth in mom-and-pop labs they sometimes did things like add color to their product to make it distinctive. A drug enforcement agent in rural Virginia told us:

> There was this one group where everything was pink, and they always had it in those pink, clear Tupperware containers with little blue lids. Everything was coming that way. . . . It looked a little wet. I never really touched it, but it didn't look powdery, kind of clay-ish. . . . Everything was pink. And now, probably since the middle or end of '07 until now, just about everything is ice. And usually, a lot of times, when we're getting it around here, the stuff, even ounces at a time it's still wet.

For purposes of public safety and health this is not insignificant. A doctor who works in an emergency room in a hospital in Oregon asked us, "Has there been anything unusual found in the crystal meth that's out there? Is it P2P or ephedrine, or something else? Because if we're having actual stabilization or a slight decrease in use, why is there a slight increase in deaths?"

For consumers of methamphetamine in the United States the changes in the industry due to the introduction of the pseudoephedrine legislation resulted in a shift in many places from the powder and paste made by local cooks to the crystal delivered by the Mexican corporate importers. As noted earlier, some of the local cooks even started adding a step to their process to transform their powder into crystal. According to a police respondent in a small city in southern Arizona they did this for business reasons, to make more money:

> Ice is just very pure meth. The meth cookers here in the United States, specifically the West Coast, California and so forth, learned that they can make ice and that they could sell their product for a lot more than they were selling it for, you know, the old peanut butter meth, the dirty meth, the P2P meth. When they learned that they could turn it into ice, they were starting to make money hand over fist. Well, all along the cartels, the Mexicans, a lot of small DTOs, they would cook meth down there as well. And a lot of the stuff was comin' over, I mean, they weren't sophisticated meth cookers. They were sending garbage across the border. I mean, you talk to the meth heads on the street around here, they'd talk about the meth, they would compare the meth the same way they do marijuana now. . . . They would say, you know, that Mexican garbage, that peanut butter meth, it's nasty. It's all different colors, different consistencies. There was no standard. But then you would hear about these guys comin' up with ice. But where was the ice coming from? That was coming from labs out of San Bernardino and Riverside, which actually were being run by Mexican nationals but they were being coached and basically instructed by Americans who knew how to cook ice. The cartels say, hey, we're gonna get in on this. And now there are essentially fewer labs in the U.S. than there used to be. And now the Mexicans are cooking all ice.

His argument suggests a dynamic between the change in the quality of the product and the way the different competitors in the methamphetamine industry operated.

The example from Arizona describes how the quality of methamphetamine was transformed after the legislation in the meth markets and methamphetamine industry with the introduction of imported meth from Mexican sources. In contrast, a police official from Illinois described how the process for making meth and consequently the quality of local meth changed even though imported methamphetamine did not come to the area. This police official from Jacksonville, Illinois, had told us the legend of Bob Paillet. In talking about Paillet he described how "back then we had the larger P2P labs, pheny12propanol, and also the red phosphorous iodine labs" until the early 1990s when these were replaced by the Nazi dope labs using a process that involved lithium or sodium metal or metal anhydrous ammonia. He explained how Paillet sold his recipe and taught this method to "literally hundreds and hundreds of individuals throughout southwest Missouri." Today, he told us, the old Nazi dope labs have been replaced by "the one-pot [shake-and-bake] method." A big difference is that with one-pot the cook "doesn't make as much methamphetamine at one time, but it's a lot quicker and a lot easier to do," though it remains dangerous to do. The point of this story is how the local methamphetamine industry, and with it the quality of local meth, changed even though, unlike other parts of the country, crystal meth imported from Mexico was not introduced in this area. The meth produced in Nazi labs has never been considered very good, so while the quality of methamphetamine produced by any process is dependent on the quality of the work of the cook making the meth, many people felt that the quality of local meth improved with the introduction of shake-and-bake. That is, with the technological changes in the way methamphetamine was being made came changes in the quality of the product as well. Obviously this change was not as dramatic as the change in areas where the local paste or powder from Nazi labs or even one-pot cooks was replaced by the crystal from the Mexican importers. Nonetheless, as described by one of the police officers we spoke to in Kentucky, today shake-and-bake meth cooks are proud of the product they make, treating it like a "secret family recipe," whereas in the old days it "could look like brown sugar, powder, they didn't care. I saw some looked like brown snot, it was actually a goo. But it tested positive."

When we specifically asked all fifty respondents about product quality during our telephone interviews, most of the detectives we spoke to said the product from Mexico was of a higher quality. A respondent from Utah believed he knew why: "The quality of the product that we see out of Mexico is such a better quality product . . . because you have people who probably have doctorates in chemistry who are working at an actual laboratory in Mexico creating this product as opposed to John the skinhead tweaker who was taught by Suzie the skinhead tweaker how to make it and has to throw away half of the batches because they're terrible."

During a telephone interview a detective in Tennessee described this transformation and how local cooks used new technologies for making meth. Whether or not the Mexican superlabs are run by scientists with degrees in chemistry, what the local cooks did allowed them to respond to the challenge of competing with the crystal meth imported from Mexico:

> Originally, it was the locally manufactured methamphetamine. The purity was very low. It was made locally by local cooks. When ice started showing up on the scene, it was imported in from Mexico . . . through Mexican gangs. They were transported in through existing drug corridors from the border. I want to say that started about 2003, 2004. That in the last year, year and a half to be safe, has changed. Increased border security and the situation that's going on in Mexico has made it much more difficult to get that product across the border and we're just not seeing that activity from those gang members here now. And [locally] they can manufacture through this shake-and-bake method of manufacturing a locally made product that has a purity level that is not as good as ice but it's really close. [The new local stuff is] probably in the 80 to 90 percent purity range. And in the previous method of manufacture, they were somewhat fairly sophisticated operations but they ran a lot of risk because there were such huge issues related to odors and things that would tip off neighbors and things of that nature. With the shake-and-bake method, they can have that in a trunk of a car. They don't run the risk of their neighbors smelling the manufacturing process like they did previously because that tipped us off a lot of times. We get calls from neighbors, "Hey, we're smelling this chemical smell," and we would go after that area and we could smell it too and it was just a matter of following your nose to where you need to be. Well, it's not that way anymore. I mean it just requires a two-liter plastic coke bottle and some time and the precursors.

So it would appear that the quality and character of methamphetamine as a product is related both to technological advances and to the social dynamics of the local markets.

One interesting thing about the introduction of the crystal or ice imported from Mexico and the paste or powder produced in mom-and-pop labs is the controversy it has created over which is better. In rural Georgia, for example, a husband and wife who both used and sold meth together believed that "ice was a lot better. It would keep you up longer. We were able to maintain somewhat of a normal life doing crank, until we started doing ice. When we started doing ice, we destroyed our life within a matter of four years." In contrast, a local sheriff in a city in Missouri, where imported meth never took hold and the mom-and-pop labs are still the main source of meth, told us: "Ice is harder to get and they [users] don't like the taste of it compared to shake-and-bake. Since the next generation [of users] has come up what I've found is that your early twenties, mid-twenties people it's all shake-and-bake. Older people coming out of prison still hold to the old anhydrous because it's all they know."

A police investigator in Virginia suggested that the perceived difference in taste or quality between home-cooked meth and meth imported from Mexico is really a difference in appearance, saying "Mexican dope looks better." In Oregon, where virtually all the methamphetamine comes from Mexico, the meth dealer we talked about earlier argues that the crystal meth from Mexico is better because it is less likely to be altered. As noted earlier, he said to us, "Crystal never gets stepped on." Not everyone agrees. In contrast, a state trooper from Indiana, where virtually all the meth used in the area is produced in local labs, said:

> The dope that they make here typically, and this doesn't happen in every lab, but most of our labs, they're not cutting the dope with something else. They're not putting baking soda in it. They're not putting MSM [methylsulfonylmethane] in it. What you're providing to people is pure dope that just came out of a cook process. When Mexican dope comes across the border from Mexico it goes to Atlanta, it goes to Detroit, it goes to Chicago, to the big dealer. The big dealer cuts it with something. It goes out to the smaller dealers. The smaller dealers bring it to South Bend, they bring it to Fort Wayne, they bring it to Indianapolis. They cut it again. So what you may be getting from your Mexican dope might be 40 percent, 50 percent methamphetamine; the rest is gonna be whatever they've

added to it. What you get from your local meth cook is all methamphetamine. . . . And it's not L-methamphetamine and it's not half D–half L. You've got D-methamphetamine in its purest form.

There is no simple answer to the question of which is better and which is purer. But for certain not all meth is equal, and the people who buy and use it know it.

COMMUNICATIONS IN THE METHAMPHETAMINE INDUSTRY

Another aspect of the culture of an industry is found in the way participants communicate with one another. For example, as has become increasingly common in other illicit drug industries, people involved in the methamphetamine industry and markets use cell phones and text messaging to communicate. Of our survey respondents, 97 percent reported that meth dealers and users in their area communicate by cell phone and 83 percent said that in their area text messaging is used.

In one small rural town in Virginia, a young man we interviewed whose only livelihood has been selling meth told us he would arrange by text message or cell phone to meet his distributor on dark country roads:

> There were two or three regular places and it was around back roads. He spoke fairly good English but, basically, we just had a couple of little phrases like "the usual." We knew that that meant four ounces and he'd know the name of a road here or there. And other than that, we didn't really have a whole lot of communication. We just set up the deal and we'd meet on the road, and a lot of times just handed off on the road, sometimes not even come to a complete stop. I had my back window down, and he throws the dope in my back window and I'd throw a lot of money in his back window. . . . [He contacted me] either by text message or call, yeah. . . . Oh, of course, of course, yeah, we had to be careful. I mean, meeting on the back road. If I had my way, he would have buried the stuff somewhere in one place and just called my phone or had a signal to call and let me know it was there, buried on the side of road in a designated spot, and then

I'd put my money in another designated spot so that I'd never be in the same spot, you know, we'll never be in the same place together.

A detective in that same area told us that meth transactions take place wherever cell phones go. Similarly, a detective from a small town in New Mexico told us about the extent and nature of their use in his area and how his department uses the seized phone for subsequent investigations:

> We seize them all the time. Every time we do a search warrant, we'd seize the cell phones and looking through the phones, asking for phones. This is for both deals in the dealer's apartment and courier sort of activity. Like they'd call and say, "Hey, I want some drugs." They'll make a meeting place like in a public place. If they know you well enough, they'll go by your house and make a delivery, but you're going to have to buy enough to make it worth their while for the trip. What we've found is that the drug pusher is contacted by several people and then he'll make one big trip and distribute it.

The developments in modern communications technology have been as important for doing business in the methamphetamine industry as they have for most other areas of social life. Respondents as far apart as Atlanta, Georgia, and Salem, Oregon, told us about cases of meth deals being set using code transmitted during an online game involving Xboxes. Others mentioned things like iPods and Skype for communicating information to set up meth deals.

The language that industry and market participants use to communicate is also part of their culture. A respondent in Seattle suggested that if we listen to conversations near a homeless shelter we would hear what he called the local "lingo" used for meth deals in that community, with different cities and different places each having their own lingo or slang. But certain words become common across the industry and across the country. This happens, for example, when a new word is needed to describe a new phenomenon that has evolved to meet a new demand in the industry. In the methamphetamine industry, smurfing is a good example of this.

In the early 1980s a television cartoon series was introduced in the United States based on a Belgian comic strip and animated film about little blue characters called smurfs. Smurfs became a cultural phenomenon and even meth users and dealers in the United States know the smurfs.

Whether it is because of the blue color of some pseudoephedrine pills or the small army of little people running around to collect cold tablets, smurfing is now the name used nationwide for people collaborating to get enough chemical for a cook to make a batch of meth for them to share. As a narcotics detective in California explained:

> Well, what we're seeing now is a lot of people doing smurfing and going to four, five, six, ten, twelve different pharmacies and getting their maximum number of cold pills. And half the time, they go with two, three, and four people so after a full day of smurfing you've got enough to make a couple or three ounces of meth. The smurfers typically aren't the people that are cooking dope. They go in and smurf and at the end of the day they meet up with whoever, either the cook or an intermediary, and he gives them whatever he's going to give them, either dope or money for their smurfing. And they go on their merry way.

A detective in Kentucky described the practice as it is used by local cooks in more detail:

> The local cooks will solicit people either through product or by paying them. They'll go out and buy all the precursors and they'll make a loop, and what I mean by a loop is they'll just take a day trip to where for example they will drive to six, seven, eight counties and go to all the Walmarts and/or drugstores in the area and buy two or three boxes of Sudafed or other supplies, precursor items and they'll bring them back to the cooks and the cooks will, you know, put together the product, do the cook, create enough to where they can use some and sell some.

Everyone we spoke with across the country knew what smurfing is and how and why it works.

In Missouri we talked with a group of detectives in a drug unit about meth in their area, an area still dominated by local mom-and-pop labs. They described to us how the local labs are using smurfing to get sufficient supplies to produce their product. What they told us demonstrates a less formal and less organized form of smurfing. The response was to a question we asked about the price of an ounce of methamphetamine in the area:

[The price of an ounce is] five boxes [laughs]. It's the currency. Nobody wants cash. They want Sudafed. That's what they want. You got people picking up people at a homeless shelter and taking them to Walmart, sending them all in to buy a box and giving them back cigarettes for it. One of the big things we're seeing here is the black community [not using meth but] buying boxes. We'll go out to Walmart and do a detail and there'll be a car full of black males or females, four or five of them, at the Walmart, and they'll just get in line to buy Sudafed.

We heard a similar account from detectives in rural Indiana concerning calls they had received from two local pharmacies:

Both of them called to say that they had a van of people, African Americans, which we don't find a lot. I think they're just buying it, they're not using it. But anyway, they came and they would come in and one by one go to the counter. They said they actually think [the people in the van] even knew when they got their shipment of pseudoephedrine, and they always came on Tuesday night. And they came in, I don't know, 10 o'clock, right before the pharmacy closed and they all marched in there and presented their IDs and left. One of the pharmacists was getting off and she went outside and saw the van and got the license plate. [The police were given the information and traced the van.] And it was a group of people living in an apartment complex in the city of St. Louis.

In Phoenix, Arizona, we were told similar stories about vans and people with false identification going to one pharmacy after another buying as much pseudoephedrine as they could buy, though in Arizona the assumption was that the vans and the people in them were connected to cartels in Mexico and the drugs were being purchased for superlabs in California.

In effect, the local labs run by local cooks are small businesses. It is not surprising that the way they use smurfing is more informal than the highly organized way that the Mexican cartels would use smurfing. In Arizona the stories we were told were about a highly organized and systematic model for smurfing operated by the Mexican drug organizations in the area. The cartels purchase vans and hire drivers who then hire groups of probably

illegal Mexican immigrants. Each of the immigrants is given several different identification cards. Then every day the van is driven across the region
from one shopping area to another where the hired help each go to different pharmacies to make as many purchases of pseudoephedrine products
as possible using as many ID cards as possible. The details may be different,
but smurfing means the same thing in both cases.

FAMILIES AND FAMILY LIFE

Another way the culture of an industry or market is experienced is
through its relationship to other social institutions. In the case of methamphetamine markets their relationship to the families of participants is
very important. We first heard stories about the involvement of families
and children in meth markets while talking to meth users and dealers in
Virginia. A mature woman who was using meth when her daughter was
thirteen years old told us that "it's a family drug." She said she herself
used meth and she knew her daughter had tried it because a dealer friend
of hers had "turned her [daughter] on to it." She told us "that's what dealers do. They sneak behind your back and get your kids" while "you're so
high you don't do the right thing to protect them." Similarly, you may
recall the words of a younger woman who we talked about earlier from
the area who when asked how she started using and dealing meth said,
"I was born into it. My mother was a dealer." The younger woman said
she started using when she was nine years old and then went on to sell
meth "during my teenage years" to support her mother, who by then
"was an addict" and could no longer operate her own meth business.
So we were not surprised during a later visit to Georgia when a narcotics detective without prompting told us how it "lights a fire under us"
when his department sees children involved in the production and sale
of methamphetamine. He said children learn from watching their parents
and joked that it's like "Grandma's recipe for famous biscuits."

Across the country we continued to find examples and hear stories
of how the participation of an individual in a meth market had an impact
on other family members, including children. For example, a woman
meth user from Oregon told us the following story:

> Well, it started in Idaho and I was married to a cook and didn't real-
> ize it. And I was taking some antidepressants and he was substituting

the methamphetamine in my capsules. It just escalated from there. My son was married to a woman in Idaho and they did not tell him that her parents were drug lords. So he had his own little thing going on over here, but he was able to rescue his kids out of that and move to Oregon. Then I had another son that was, of course, had different personalities and had carried himself in different ways, and he had moved here with my mom and dad. And unfortunately, he decided that he could handle the whole Portland area and [it] resulted in him murdering somebody in my mom and dad's yard. And then from there, I had a daughter. She went to a different level of the drug use [specifically, intravenous use]. Slamming is what it's called. That took her to a different level. There's levels of how you can do this drug [meth], and it also carries you to a different level of mental state too and how you physically see it and it's really sad.

Also in Oregon a drug treatment counselor told us, "We're treating second- and third-generation families here now. Over the last fifteen years we're seeing children and even grandchildren coming in for treatment." In rural Kentucky a police officer told us about a case he had "where a bunch of parents would get together on the weekends and sit around and play cards and let the kids play while they cook their meth. It was just for personal use. They just enjoyed doing it, it was fun." In Carbondale, Illinois, a respondent told us that the youngest meth user he knows is age nine, and was turned on by his sister, age thirteen, and she was turned on by her parents. In El Paso, Texas, a respondent told us that "the family that cooks together stays together."

Exposing families and children to meth markets exposes them to the dangers of those markets and the people who populate them. Depending on the type of market, they become subject to things such as the noxious fumes and chemical explosions of mom-and-pop labs and the poor hygiene and related infectivity of meth users. Perhaps of greater concern, children and other family members are exposed to neglect and domestic violence. According to a member of an interagency drug crime law enforcement team we spoke with in Indiana, exposing children and families to the dangers of meth production and use is an emerging problem: "It was taboo in 1996 to cook in your house. Everybody cooked out in their barn or they cooked out in a shed or they cooked out in a river cabin. And then by the early 2000s it was okay to cook in the house as long as the kids weren't home. And then by the mid-2000s it was all right to cook in the house if the kids were home, as long as the kids were in their room. And now it's shake-and-bake in the car while you're with them. So they're socialized as kids to see this as acceptable behavior." Similarly a respondent in Kentucky told us how parents sit around their house while their children are "crawling around with the jars of ether and stuff" that the parents use to make meth. In Indiana a police officer explained that when children are removed from homes where methamphetamine was being made all of their belongings, including clothes and toys, are contaminated and have to be left behind. We heard repeatedly around the country that today this type of neglect is a common problem.

In crack cocaine markets most of the violence related to the drug was the product of attempts to resolve market disputes. With meth markets to the extent there is violence it is domestic rather than market related. As a detective from a city in New Mexico told us, "I wouldn't say so much a competition [among meth dealers] as the violence we're seeing is just [personal or within families. It is not] they're not playing well together or rip-offs versus, you know, you're selling in my area. We saw that [stealing or territorial disputes] more with the crack trade than with the meth trade." That was the story we heard about meth market violence across the country. The competition is a business competition with disputes being resolved maybe by threats but mostly by pricing rather than violent actions. Domestic violence and neglect are another story.

In all the regions we visited when we asked about violence we were told about violence involving families and children. When asked about domestic rather than market violence, the detective from New Mexico said: "It's the most violent drug because they have paranoia. And the other thing is trying to keep up their habit, they're depleting the family budget and of course the family doesn't like it, whether it's the brother, the mother, the wife, and so they argue with them and they wind up in physical altercations, and of course we get called, the police." The detective from New Mexico explained the damage methamphetamine does to families:

It ruins people. I mean, the crack does too, but the methamphetamine deteriorates people's health, it ruins families. I bet everybody that's hooked on meth does not have a family anymore—mother, father, grandfather, wife, children—nobody wants anything to do with them because they can't control them. These people get violent. After a while, they even consider themselves homeless. They're sleeping out in cars, wherever they can stay but they don't cut the habit. It's just a horrible thing. And sometimes, they get violent enough to shoot or stab other people and they get into that type of thing. The only thing that sometimes helps them is when we lock them up and they get a chance to dry out and realize what they've done but the majority of times they go right back. There are very few that have not come back and of the ones I know, they had gone back and that's terrible.

Similarly, when asked about domestic violence and neglect, a detective from Tennessee told us about his own experience:

Child endangerment is a huge problem—we have more children in state's custody as a result of methamphetamine. I have a three-year-old step grandson that I've had since he was five months old and it's a direct result of meth. He's three and a half years old now. And that is very, very, very common. We have a lot of young children, parents, and other family members [similarly impacted negatively] and you can attribute that to methamphetamine use.

A detective in Utah illustrates how children become neglected in meth households: "We got a lot of domestic issues, a lot of child neglect. Many, many of our search warrants on meth dealers are served where they have small children in the home, they're using meth in the home, they're cooking the meth with the children in the home. The drug just has such an effect on you psychologically that nobody can get along with you for long and you're going to break and have those mood swings and aggression so we see meth taking quite a toll on the family." When asked about domestic violence related to methamphetamine in his area, a police drug unit member in Georgia said, "That's rampant, that's crazy around here. Sixty to seventy percent of all personal crime is meth related." A family service provider in Virginia told us, "This is all new, it's really scary."

In a small city in Oregon we talked with a large group of family service providers and drug treatment counselors at a residential treatment facility. They told us about meth-using women who gave birth to children and then lost them in a particularly unfortunate way:

> In the last three years we saw a definite increase in Hispanic men having babies with Caucasian women, having babies together. And the woman is totally off the hook [out of control] on her meth use. And she goes to the hospital and they deliver the baby and DHS [Department of Human Services] gets called because the baby tests positive for methamphetamine use. Then what happens is because the father is clean, he is the first one to be looked at as a potential person to take the child. The fathers [are not users but] they're selling. They're drinking alcohol and smoking pot. Half of our mother and children population here [at the Center] would fit into that category. It's been an interesting trend. And you know, they [the fathers] have their whole family here that kind of backs them up. Then the woman who is in treatment and trying to do what she needs to do, we'll see him [the father] totally turn his back on her. They're like, "You're a bad woman. You failed. I'm gonna get the child back and go to Mexico with it." You hear that a lot.

Not all fathers send the child back to Mexico, but they do become the legal guardian and cut the mother off from having a relationship with her child. In another city in Oregon we met the Mexican meth dealer who told us with pride that he is a single father with custody of four children, all from different mothers. The mothers are meth users and legally considered unfit to care for their children. He is a meth dealer but not a user so legally he is capable of being a father and has sole custody of the children.

CULTURE

The two women discussed earlier in this chapter who were methamphetamine users living in Virginia came from small communities located in the historic Shenandoah Valley. The younger woman lived near a small city called Staunton. Staunton is at the intersection of two interstate highways, I-81 and I-64, and about 170 miles northeast of Galax. Located in Augusta County, Staunton is the birthplace of the city manager form of government popular today in many cities in the United States, and also the birthplace of President Woodrow Wilson. Given its strategic location at the meeting of two interstate highways and its proximity to recreational areas such as the Shenandoah National Park, Staunton has some appeal for business and tourism. Of the population of almost twenty-four thousand people living in Staunton almost 83 percent are white, 12 percent are black, and only about 2 percent are of Hispanic origin. Income and housing values are not particularly high, but most everyone who wants to be employed has a job. So there are not that many people in Staunton who are methamphetamine users, but there are some and unfortunately some of those who are bring meth into their family life.

Culture to a large extent is passed along across generations through families, so when an important family member, especially a father or a mother, is involved with methamphetamine it can get passed from one generation to the next. Earlier in this chapter and in the last we quoted the younger woman from Staunton, Virginia, who told us "I was born into it" when asked about how she became involved with the use and business of methamphetamine. Her story shows how the stuff that makes up the world of methamphetamine can easily and seamlessly be passed from a mother to a daughter in the natural course of family life.

As she tells the story, when she was a young girl her mother was addicted to meth and other members of her family were also using and selling. She first started using by herself when she was nine years old and started selling when she was a teenager "to take care of my mother." When we asked her how she felt about using meth at that age, she said simply that "it was fun" being a kid going to elementary school high on meth. She says she used it every day, smoking it, never injecting. Back then the methamphetamine available in the area was crank, a pink powder. There was no ice in the area at the time. You burn the cut off [eliminate the additive used as filler], you roll it on aluminum foil, and you burn it on the aluminum foil. Her mother did not smoke meth but rather she "shot up." So how, we asked, did she learn to smoke it? "A friend of mine taught me how to smoke it," she told us. Her mother was "giving it to me," but they each used it in their own way.

When her mother got too sick from using to continue to support them as a dealer, as a teenager the young woman found her own supplier and began selling it herself. She started by hanging out on the avenue where she had friends who knew people who knew people and introduced her to people who were selling. She got a job as a runner. In that way she sold their product for the people she got it from, had some to sell to her own customers, and she had her own product left over to smoke. We asked how much she was running. She gave a short laugh and said "a lot." She could sell an eight ball for $400, she told us.

When she was still a teenager her mother was arrested and she was taken away by social services and put in a juvenile facility. Her father fought to get her back. He too had been a meth user, sharing in the pink powder that she and her mother used. But he was ready to stop. The way she tells it, he fought "through hell and high water" and he won her back. In Virginia it was not easy for a father to win custody of a daughter, but her father "did everything he had to," including giving up methamphetamine and any other drug he had been using.

Despite the best efforts of her father, when she was seventeen she "got mixed in with the wrong crowd" and got back into dealing drugs. She was a teenager and felt she had nothing to lose. But she did. She got arrested. She is convinced that she got set up by the police, and ultimately she was charged with a felony. At age twenty-three at the time of the interview by her own account she has been clean, no methamphetamine, for five years. From all the other people we have spoken with about methamphetamine, assuming that what she said about being clean for five years is true, it is a big deal. When we asked how she did it she told us it was because she had a daughter, a two year old. Her daughter, she told us, is her life and she "would never choose any drug over her." The father of her baby still uses meth, along with other drugs, so he is out of their life. She worries that her daughter might find drugs herself one day, and that concerns her. These are not her words, but she is hopeful that the cultural transmission of methamphetamine use in her family ends with her generation and never moves on to the next, her own daughter.

CHAPTER 6

Meth Markets and the Methamphetamine Industry in the United States

In the United States the methamphetamine industry is the sum of all the means and methods that are used for the manufacture, distribution, and sale of methamphetamine as the product moves from producers to consumers. It is the sum of all the things the people who are involved with methamphetamine do and how they relate to one another and how they give meaning to their actions and relationships. Early in the twenty-first century the methamphetamine industry was confronted by a huge challenge to its future when both the federal and state governments introduced legislation to curtail access to a principal ingredient necessary for the production of methamphetamine, which itself of course was already not a legal product. In this book we have considered the impact including the unintended consequences of that challenge. One of our main findings has been that the industry has successfully adapted to the challenge and effectively has reinvented itself.

You may recall that at the start of our study of methamphetamine markets in America we conducted a survey of almost fourteen hundred police departments in a variety of cities and towns and counties in all fifty states. A major finding of that survey was that in the years following the introduction of the restrictive legislation on both the federal and state levels, two types of methamphetamine markets emerged to sustain and even revitalize the methamphetamine industry. Analyzing our survey data we determined that different places had different configurations of market types, often more than one. Given the inability to obtain necessary ingredients locally, we found that some places had primarily import markets mostly with the crystallized form of methamphetamine known as ice coming from Mexico or produced in the United States by Mexican cartels. In other places local manufacturers conceived of new ways to obtain the necessary ingredients, generally some form of the process called smurfing, and new ways to produce product using different mixes of ingredients, notably the method known as shake-and-bake, and were able to sustain the local businesses that were producing small amounts of methamphetamine for local users.

Once we analyzed our findings from our survey we proceeded to interview narcotics detectives in fifty jurisdictions and then to visit, observe, and talk to people in five regions of the country. One thing we learned from doing this was the importance of looking deep into the details of what we saw and what people told us to better understand what was happening in places with active methamphetamine markets and why it was happening. Throughout this book we have provided rich detail through our accounts and depictions of what we heard, saw, and experienced and through the quotations from the people with whom we spoke. To provide a fuller understanding of the social worlds we observed and the evolution of methamphetamine markets we explored in places that have primarily one or the other of the two different types of market organization or some combination of both, below we tell the stories of two different places each representing one of these types. These stories are intended to illustrate the different ways that the social activity of the people who participate in one type of market or another is shaped by their experience and relationships with other participants in a meaningful and productive way.

THE STORY OF A MARKET PRIMARILY
SUPPLIED BY IMPORTED METH

Tacoma is located on the Puget Sound in the state of Washington in the northwestern part of the United States on the I-5 Interstate corridor not far from the Pacific Ocean. Tacoma is less than forty miles south of Seattle, Washington, and about 140 miles north of Portland, Oregon. According to the 2010 Census there were 198,397 people living in Tacoma, about 65 percent of them white, 12 percent black, and about 11 percent of Hispanic ancestry, mostly from Mexico. According to a city website (City of Tacoma, Washington 2013), the economy in the city appears to be doing well with a growing high-technology industry and an established "diverse economy strong in agricultural and forest products, manufacturing, health care, financial and professional services, and the military." Nonetheless among a small segment of the local population there is an interest in methamphetamine.

While we were in the Pacific Northwest we spent some time talking with a group of local law enforcement officers and officials whose job it is to deal with illicit drug markets in the Tacoma area. When we asked about the mom-and-pop methamphetamine labs in the area, we were told "they're definitely down. I think that this year we haven't had any what we would consider to be an active lab. Last year we had one or two. The year prior to that, the numbers would be the same. It really dropped off in '05 or early '06. They went from, I don't know the exact numbers, but to include dumpsites and active labs from in the *hundreds* [emphasis in his voice] to what we're experiencing now, basically nothing." In recent years the numbers are so low that there has been talk among policymakers of disbanding the police unit designated to deal with the hazards of local meth labs. If the local labs were all gone we wondered whether there were still people using methamphetamine and if so where it was coming from.

The drug industry, according to what we were told, is cyclical. Local labs could come back to the area one day. Explaining why they believe the local labs were not present at the time one of the officers told us that it was related to the restrictions placed on access to necessary ingredients, including not only pseudoephedrine but also anhydrous ammonia. Also, around that time a lot of the local cooks were arrested and convicted, "doing a five-year minimum sentence" in prison "for unlawful manufacture of a controlled substance."

This does not mean that all the local production is gone. The police know that there are still a few people out there making meth. Smurfers, they said, "will go around to the different pharmacies and obtain the precursor, the pseudoephedrine, two boxes at a time. And they'll provide either the tablets or the extracted pseudo to the cook. Another person in the business model might provide the anhydrous. And somebody will eventually cook it up. And then they'll have people that they'll distribute it to." But this type of production only produces small yields and only serves a small number of users, and in any case "has really dropped off."

Most of the methamphetamine in the area at the time of our visit was imported. As one of the police officers we were talking to said, "With the drug cartels, it's basically all coming from Mexico." They recognize that methamphetamine is still a problem and some people in the area are still using it, but "they're just not cookin' it in their back garage." They assume there has been a flow of methamphetamine from Mexico for the past twenty or thirty years, but when the legislation was enacted to control access to pseudoephedrine the price of meth in the area "skyrocketed." According to one officer, "An ounce of methamphetamine costs more than an ounce of cocaine." That was new for the area. An ounce of cocaine was costing $700 to $800, considered a good deal, and an ounce of methamphetamine was costing between $1,200 and $1,500. He concluded, "It's pricey."

Compared to the powder produced in local labs, the methamphetamine from Mexico is the crystal form known as ice. One officer told us that even though people think the ice is purer "it's really not." He explained how it involves one more step to make ice. The superlabs in Mexico, he told us, make big ice crystals since they discovered that users think it is higher grade stuff. So now in Tacoma they are "seeing more crystal methamphetamine."

We asked how the ice market worked, how it was being distributed. "Person to person," we were told. But you cannot buy methamphetamine in Tacoma on a street corner. You buy it "in private homes in or public meeting locations. But usually a user has to know a seller. You can't go up to a street corner and hit somebody up for crystal meth." We asked about whether or not the ice business appeared to have a hierarchy. "We see a lot of Mexican runners," we were told. "There's a hierarchy there. We locally don't get into the upper levels. But we will buy methamphetamine quite often from a typical runner. And that runner might be one of three or four that works for a contact, and that contact has his source. And the source has his source. So, it's predominantly being distributed by Hispanics. There's no doubt about that."

Next we asked about the users. One of the police officers said, "I would say, whites." The Mexican runners normally are not using meth. "Normally," we were told, "they're just collecting the cash and they're giving it to their source or any proceeds that they might make they're using it to subsidize their standard of living: rent, food, clothing, or sending it back to family in Mexico." The police admit that they really do not have the ability to reach many of the runners as informants. Most of them are in the United States illegally but are less concerned with being deported than they are with what they believe will happen to their families in Mexico if they speak to the police. The world in which they live and the business in which they participate "turns out to be a real small world," so they are "not willing to jeopardize their family." And in any case, if they are deported they know that the cartels will arrange to send them back so they can return to work.

One of the last questions we asked the local police was whether they would be surprised to see an article in the local newspaper or on television one day that there was a large Mexican cartel operating in their area. They seemed to be surprised that we would even ask. But they would not be surprised to hear that such was the case, they told us.

THE STORY OF A MARKET PRIMARILY SUPPLIED BY HOMEGROWN METH

St. Louis is the second largest city in Missouri located centrally in the Midwestern region of the United States near the border between Missouri and Illinois (City of Saint Louis, Missouri 2013). In 2010 the U.S. Census counted 319,294 people living in the city. Of those 44 percent were white, 49 percent black, and less than 4 percent were of Hispanic ancestry. The local economy is based on service and manufacturing industries, trade and transportation, and tourism. The economic recovery of the city and the surrounding area continues to lag behind the rest of the country, largely based on slow job recovery in the region. Nonetheless there is reason to believe that most people living in the area live legitimate and productive lives. But still there is some evidence that some people are involved in the business and use of methamphetamine.

St. Louis was one of the places we visited during our national tour of regions around the country to study methamphetamine markets. There we met and spoke with members of the local metropolitan police and others from a regional interagency methamphetamine law enforcement team. As we discussed earlier in this book, the methamphetamine markets in the Midwest continue to be based primarily on local production rather than imports from Mexico. So in St. Louis one of the first questions we asked was about what happened after the pseudoephedrine laws were passed.

We were told that before the legislation there was a "huge" local lab problem in the area. The laws in 2004 and 2005 were intended to control that, but did not. The cooks, according to one of the people we were talking with, "figured out the process." Apparently the cooks started going to fifteen stores in one day to get what they needed, then continued to adapt as the risks of getting caught or getting "busted" increased. We asked about the types of labs in the area in those days. "Years ago they were anhydrous labs," we were told. "Now we're seeing more one-pots."

Another police officer, who had been certified to do this work for a long time and had been to "almost eight hundred labs, mostly rural," told us more about how the local cooks now using one-pot to make meth adapted to the restrictions placed on key ingredients they needed:

> Before limits were put on it, pseudoephedrine was easy to get. You know, one person went out and got thirty boxes. Now thirty people go out and [each] buy one box. Now the difference is pseudoephedrine's become the currency of clandestine drug labs. It's worth $50 to $75 a box or a half a gram of meth, and it's basically become the currency of meth. The effect of that was a couple of things. And I've interviewed a lot of people who've told me this, they started out with the idea they were gonna make a hundred bucks a month or so off of pseudoephedrine. They weren't users. Or they were very minimal users. Well, before long the next thing you know the [cook tells them] well, I don't got fifty bucks for your pseudo but I'll give you a quarter gram of meth. Well, he's saving twenty-five to fifty bucks by doin' that and he's hookin' them. So this whole pseudoephedrine thing it started out looking like a good thing, but it ended up causin' a big black market for pseudoephedrine and also expanded the usage. More people are using. That's the difference to me.

The person telling us this story explained that he mostly works in rural areas, so he could not say if ice was being used in the city, but some of his colleagues were working meth cases involving ice and imports. Still, in the first six months of the year during which we were talking to him, 2011, there were 741 local meth lab cases he had to deal with. Of those the vast majority, he said, were one-pots.

Continuing the story of the local labs in the rural areas around St. Louis, the officer said: "It used to be people saved up their pills and did one or two cooks a month. Now they get two boxes of pills and do a cook. So there are a lot more labs for the simple fact that instead of them doin' one process twice a month, they're doin' it every day or every other day, one-pots." With the limits on access to pseudoephedrine and with pseudoephedrine being the currency for buying meth, various forms of smurfing have been introduced in the area. One officer gave us an example: "You got people pickin' up ten or fifteen people at the homeless shelter and takin' them to Walmart. Send them all in to buy a box and give 'em a pack of cigarettes." Another example came up when one officer said, "One of the big changes we're seein' here is the black community." At that moment another yelled out, "Bingo!" As noted earlier, we had heard this mentioned elsewhere a few times but not often. Across the country methamphetamine has not been popular among black people, specifically those who are users of other illicit drugs. You may recall a case we described earlier where a drug dealer in North Carolina was trying to convince a group of people buying a large amount of cocaine from him to take on consignment a large quantity of methamphetamine to open the market in their city in the Middle Atlantic region where there were a lot of drug users but not a lot of meth use. The deal fell through. A large proportion of both the overall population and the population of illicit drug users in the target city were black and were not interested in methamphetamine. So how and why were black people in St. Louis suddenly interested in methamphetamine? We asked if they were involved in using or were they involved in the business. Neither. The officer who originally brought it up told us the interest of black people living in St. Louis in methamphetamine was "buying boxes." He explained, in words we quoted earlier, "We go out to Walmart and do a detail and there'll be a car full of black males or females, which normally you won't see. They'll go out there and there'll be four or five of 'em in the Walmart and they'll just get in line to buy pseudoephedrine. You didn't see that earlier as a rule, but you do see it now."

Recalling the cook we met in a jail in western Georgia after he blew himself up trying to make six bottles of one-pot at the same time, we asked about the extent to which there were explosions and fatalities in the area around St. Louis where there were so many one-pot operations: "In the past twenty-four months we've had more injuries from meth labs than we've had in all the years up to this point. We've had some fatalities with explosions, and fires [including] a couple with shrapnel."

We also asked about the quality of the one-pot meth being cooked for the local market, given all the conflicting stories we had been told about the low quality of P2P or Red-P meth and ice being better and ice not really being better. One of the officers told us, "I think it's what they get used to." Another continued, "Most of the people, you ask them about ice around here, most of the locals around here they don't handle it much. It's a little harder to get. They don't like the taste of the ice versus shake-and-bake."

Interestingly, there is a generational element to the question of quality and preference in the St. Louis area. One officer told us, "Since the next generation has come up, you know, in their early twenties to mid-twenties, that's all they are is shake-and-bake." He explained that "the older generation" of meth users from ten years ago or so remain interested in anhydrous or Nazi meth. In contrast, "the younger generation" prefers shake-and-bake. They express concern about the risks associated with making anhydrous dope. They are not talking about the hazards of chemical waste or explosion, which are there for both methods, but rather the risk of getting caught for stealing anhydrous ammonia from tanks. To make shake-and-bake everything you need is easy to get. The officer explained that for one-pot you can "buy everything you need in a store or walk into a house. I mean, it's all common stuff. They can conceal it better. They don't have to worry about getting caught stealing. They don't have to worry about havin' a leak. They don't have to worry about any of that stuff. So [although] a lot of your old cooks stay with [anhydrous], everybody else is just tryin' the one-pot."

What we learned about social status is also interesting as it relates to cooking methamphetamine in local labs in the St. Louis area. Unlike the people who are at the upper levels of the methamphetamine corporate importing enterprises run by the Mexican cartels, the people involved with methamphetamine cooking in local labs more often than not do not have a lot of money. Also they do not have a lot of education or work experience. In the legitimate world of social life and commerce they tend to be treated poorly and are not highly respected. As it turns out, historically in the local meth labs in the area they have had a similar experience. As explained to us by one of the police officers in St. Louis, "In the old days, the cook was the man!" The users were disrespected by the cooks. They were treated badly by the cooks when they came around scrounging for a quarter of a gram. One officer told us, "The buyer might get stuck buying something that's mostly baby laxative and get treated bad while he's doin' it." According to what we were told, the cooks in those days got addicted not only to meth but to being cooks. They too came from poor backgrounds and had little respect in legitimate society, so being a meth cook empowered them, giving them a sense of accomplishment and success they probably had never experienced elsewhere. Of course not all cooks were equally highly regarded. Unfortunately for the anhydrous Nazi method cooks, despite their higher status among their users they had low status among meth cooks. According to the people we were talking to, the Red-P cooks, who were using real glassware and more complicated chemical formulas to make their meth, looked down on the anhydrous Nazi method cooks. Whether or not the Red-P was better than the anhydrous meth in quality is open to question, but the process was more complicated so the status hierarchy was established. To make matters worse for the anhydrous cooks, things changed some with the introduction of one-pot. At that point given the ingredients needed and the process involved almost anyone could become a cook.

It was clear from what we learned from the police we spoke to in St. Louis, who are responsible for enforcing the laws involving the illegal manufacture, sale, and use of methamphetamine in the area, they know a lot about the problem in their area and what might be done to address it. But unfortunately there is not much they can do. As one told us, "Under the pseudoephedrine laws we know who's buying the stuff, but we do not have the time or resources to track it down."

GOING FORWARD

Something we noted in the last chapter was that when it comes to methamphetamine production and distribution in the United States Oregon is a particularly interesting state. In federal law and in the laws of many states there are restrictions placed on the purchase of cold medicines that contain pseudoephedrine, a chemical widely used in making methamphetamine. Oregon is only one of two states (the other being Mississippi) where pseudoephedrine is legally a prescription drug, requiring a written order from a doctor to purchase medications that contain it. In other states, especially in regions such as the Midwest where almost all methamphetamine comes from local lab production, law enforcement officials have taken note. For example, a member of an interagency drug crime law enforcement team in Indiana told us:

> We know what the answer to the problem is, but the [pharmaceutical] industry doesn't wanna hear it. This is not a socioeconomic problem, it's not a drug problem, it's a matter of money. The answer to this problem has been staring us in the face since 1976. You take pseudoephedrine and ephedrine out of the mix, this problem goes away. Oregon shows that. Mississippi shows that. It's frustrating. It's cost us billions and trillions of dollars of tax money and we're locking up the same people we lock up every week because it's the most addictive drug known to man. And if we were allowed to do what we need to do it would end tomorrow throughout the United States. Just make pseudoephedrine a prescription drug and this ends.

Whether or not the pharmaceutical industry is to blame and whether or not methamphetamine "is the most addictive drug known to man" are both open questions. But the Oregon experience does show that while making pseudoephedrine a prescription drug may close down local lab production, it does not diminish the demand for methamphetamine nor does it shut down the industry. In Medford, a small city in southern Oregon not far from the California border, a drug treatment counselor told us that the day the law passed a meth cook sitting in her treatment group laughed and said to her, "We've already figured out how to make [meth] without [pseudo]." She continued, "They in essence [were] removing an oxygen molecule or something, and they were saying they were using something else. They can put this in, and drain cleaner or something. Before the ink even dried on the bill, they got it." Perhaps even more to the point, markets grew all over the state that distributed and sold methamphetamine imported by the same large businesses in Mexico that had been importing other drugs.

Much has changed in the methamphetamine industry in America over the past decade or so since the introduction of the federal and state legislation to inhibit the sale of necessary precursor chemicals for making methamphetamine. There are now new types of markets, such as the import markets, and new business models, such as smurfing. The favored form of the product itself has changed in many places from powder or paste to crystal. In this book we discussed the evolution of the industry and its markets and provided details and examples to illustrate what happened and why. We conclude by clarifying the outcomes and consequences of the transition of the markets and the progression of the industry.

In any social organization individuals respond and react to things that happen around them. When rules change and customary practices for achieving objectives and goals become more difficult or even impossible, the people who are striving to reach those objectives and goals will find another way to do so. In law enforcement, for example, when the police introduce a new program or practice to stop a certain type of criminal activity or behavior, criminal law violators who engage in that activity or behavior find another way to accomplish it. In the methamphetamine industry, if you think of it as an industry, the introduction of legislation to restrict access to precursor chemicals used to make methamphetamine in local mom-and-pop labs resulted in the invention of new practices, notably things like smurfing and icing (as described earlier, the process of converting powder methamphetamine to crystal methamphetamine using acetone), and the introduction or at least expansion of different business organizations or models, notably the production of methamphetamine in superlabs and the importation of methamphetamine to communities where local mom-and-pop labs had been forced to shut down. On a local level, both police and methamphetamine dealers described this to us as a game. A narcotics detective in Ohio explained: "Well, the controlling of the precursors of course makes it harder. I think maybe for the first time the U.S. government is a little bit ahead of the game when it comes to that because they are making it harder for the manufacturer to do what he's doing. Of course, they'll always come up with another way, just like they've done every other thing to get around the controls and then the government reacts to that." Similarly, a detective from California described it more graphically when he said:

It's like playing checkers or chess—we make a move to counter, to investigate them, and they counter that move, and it's basically back and forth. Right now, the state-of-the-art thing is wiretaps so that's where it's going. A wiretap is obviously where you listen to their phone lines. Well, they've become aware that that's how we're getting the big seizures and that's how we're identifying these big players so what they're doing now is they've gone to drop the phones every week. So every week, they got to get a new number. You have to get up on a new line. And text messages, what they don't know is we can still get those. They haven't figured that one out yet.

And a methamphetamine dealer from Virginia told us, "Say you get a phone call. The way we do it, we use two different cell phones. You have your dope cell phone and you have your regular cell phone because there are cell phones that the police cannot track."

On the broadest level the methamphetamine industry in America responded to the pseudoephedrine legislation with two major developments: the smurfing innovation and the development of import methamphetamine markets. A narcotics detective from Tennessee described in more detail how smurfing is a way of getting around the legislation:

> The [precursor laws] have helped to some degree, but when you can cross jurisdictional boundaries—and I'll just use this as an example. We have a county that adjoins ours that they have their Walmart. Their local Walmart has banned the sale of pseudoephedrine, which is the main precursor. So what we're seeing now is those cooks from that county are coming in carloads. And even though you're going in and you're having to sign for—in Tennessee, they're required to sign for when you buy, say, Sudafed, on a log—and they'll go in and buy it. And then their buddy that was in the car with them will go and buy their limit and then the next buddy that was in the car with them will go and buy their limit and then they'll take all of their cold medication back home and cook up methamphetamine. And so there are ways to circumvent that—but even with the logs, and we use those logs to prosecute promotion of methamphetamine, they can figure out a way to do it. They can go to Walmart, they can go to Walgreens, they can go to the mom-and-pop drugstore. And even though you have the logs that are required by law and you can put the pieces of the puzzle together and see, okay, these guys met the statutory requirement for promotion of methamphetamine manufacture, it takes time to do that.

As described in an earlier chapter in more detail, smurfing was an important innovation but was not the only response by dealers to the legislation. The other outcome of the effort to control the production of methamphetamine in local labs that helped to keep the methamphetamine industry profitable and productive was the growth of superlabs and the importation of methamphetamine from Mexico. A narcotics detective from Utah said:

> I'd say when the labs here were hit so hard, the Mexicans came right into that vacuum. I think before they may have been only in cocaine and heroin and Mexican marijuana, but now they've been able to infiltrate in for the meth market. And because they actually live here and now own property here, they can do all of their wire transfers and remittals. As soon as they get a portion of money, they're sending it to Mexico. It's a very lucrative business so [when the legislation was passed it] created quite a vacuum and they filled it. And they will continue to, I think. I don't think [local mom-and-pop] labs will make a comeback unless a new process is created or new precursors are discovered.

And the result was not only a new way to deliver the product to market but a change in quality that might have benefited the dealers and users more than the people and agencies trying to control them. For example, a detective from Arizona said, "Mexican cartel [meth] quality went up. It was a lot better—you could take a look at a home thing and it would be tannish, ugly, yellowish color meth. And then you look at the Mexican cartel meth, and at first it was yellowish glass, and within six months it was so pure, sometimes I thought it was broken glass, shards of glass." Although not everyone agreed it really was better, it looked better and was marketed as better.

This book offers a view of the methamphetamine industry and methamphetamine markets in America from a broad sociological perspective. It is based on findings from a four-year study of methamphetamine markets across the country, including visits to local markets in a variety of cities, towns, and rural communities. Our findings differentiate communities with different types of markets and different mixes of market type, including the small mom-and-pop local lab businesses and those run by local representatives of large businesses importing methamphetamine to the area through national and international conglomerates.

From our study we learned that to understand and explain the social order and organization of methamphetamine markets in America, their interpersonal and organizational dynamics, and their impact on people and communities across the country, it is necessary to view the markets conceptually as social organizations that meet a demand for a particular product in local communities and operationally as components of a well-run and profitable industry that is being transformed to meet continuing demand for its product. To better understand illicit drug markets there are two important messages for policymakers, practitioners, and social researchers.

First, drug markets are social organizations and social organizations are integral parts of larger and more comprehensive social phenomena. Methamphetamine markets as social organizations do not exist in isolation. So things that happen in the broader social environment of which those markets are a part, such as the economy and the family and even language, do have consequences for the markets.

Second, methamphetamine markets are organized and operate in different ways in different places around the country, but from the broadest and most meaningful perspective they are all part of a larger methamphetamine industry that is not only national but international as well. And that industry and hence those markets are driven not only by economic and political forces but also by sociological forces that provide norms and values for structured social activity, interpersonal social interaction and relationships, and cultural artifacts, symbols, standards, and patterns for behavior. To adequately understand and explain methamphetamine markets and then be able to effectively address related challenges, not only the research and theory but more important the public policies, programs, and practices that address the public health and public safety problems associated with methamphetamine markets need to be grounded not only in economic and political principles but in sociological ones as well.

APPENDIX: THE STUDY OF THE DYNAMICS OF METHAMPHETAMINE MARKETS

THIS APPENDIX PROVIDES a more technical discussion of the research we conducted to learn the story of meth markets and the methamphetamine industry in America. Some of what is described here was discussed in earlier chapters.

In 2007 the National Institute on Drug Abuse (NIDA) and the National Institute of Justice (NIJ) released a solicitation for proposals to conduct research under a Joint NIDA-NIJ Initiative for Research on Retail Drug Markets. This book is based on findings from a study funded by NIDA through that joint initiative (NIDA Grant Number R21DA024391).

From 2007 to 2011 we conducted a mixed methods study of the dynamics of methamphetamine markets in America (Brownstein et al. 2012a, 2012b; Taylor et al. 2011a, 2011b). In social science research particular methods are used to design studies that allow for the conceptualization, understanding, and explanation of social experience as an empirical reality (Kaplan 1964; Lazarsfeld and Rosenberg 1955). Different methods are appropriate depending on what is being studied and the questions being asked. For example, when the subject of the study is regarded as an object then quantitative methods, which attend to relationships among discrete variables that are precisely defined and measured, are most effective; when the object of study is regarded as a subject then qualitative methods, which attend to meanings of and commonalities among broadly conceptualized phenomena, are most effective (compare Ragin and Amoroso 2011). Although quantitative and qualitative social science research methods are methodologically, theoretically, and philosophically distinctive, social scientists today are more likely than in the past to conduct mixed methods studies (Creswell and Plano Clark 2011; Johnson and Onwuegbuzie 2004; Small 2011). Contemporary mixed methods studies integrate methods in meaningful and productive ways rather than merely combining them in a fixed and established order, as was more common in the case of what used to be called multi-methods studies (Faules 1982; Jick 1979). For example, in multi-methods studies qualitative methods were most often assigned an exploratory role in preparation for subsequent quantitative data collection and analysis (Duffy 1987; Morgan 1998; Spergel 1961). For this study of methamphetamine markets a mixed methods design allowed for a more integrated and productive three-stage approach involving the collection and analysis of quantitative data from a national survey of police agencies in an exploratory role to inform two subsequent stages of qualitative data collection and analysis.

Getting Started

Our study was intended and designed to gain a better understanding of how illicit retail methamphetamine markets were organized and operated in different places across the United States. The aim of the study expanded as it became clear that local methamphetamine markets do not operate in isolation, but nonetheless our focus remained on understanding and being able to explain the markets and their place in the larger methamphetamine industry through the experience and perspectives of the people directly involved in them in one way or another. Consequently our goal was to be able to collect qualitative data that would allow us to understand and explain methamphetamine markets and the methamphetamine industry as a social phenomenon with its meaning given and its form constructed by market and industry participants (compare Bogdan and Taylor 1975; Brownstein 1983; Denzin and Lincoln 2011; Glaser and Strauss 1967). But before we could determine what local markets to study or to whom we should talk to about them, we needed to determine where those markets were located and to learn something about both the common and distinctive characteristics of markets in different places.

To learn where to find meth markets and what types of markets were operating in what places, we began our study with an exploratory screening survey of police agencies across the country. We followed that with open-ended and in-depth telephone interviews with narcotics police in selected departments, and finally with site visits to selected communities in selected regions around the country. The site visits were the core of our study in that they gave us the opportunity to learn about the markets from the people whose lives intersected on a regular basis with the markets we were studying. Over the course of about a year we visited more than twenty-eight cities and towns and rural communities in five regions of the country (Southeast, Middle Atlantic, Midwest, Southwest, and Pacific Northwest). We talked not only with local police but also with local and regional public health and safety officials, drug treatment and prevention workers, family service providers, methamphetamine users and dealers, and other people who know about meth markets in their community and region. We walked or drove through areas where local people told us we would find houses belonging to methamphetamine users and dealers or places where methamphetamine was made or bought and sold. We attended community events to hear local citizens talk about methamphetamine in their community and its impact on personal and social life in the area. We toured the U.S.-Mexico border guided by a member of the U.S. Border Patrol following the fences and river and stopping at a border crossing in an area where methamphetamine was known to have crossed the border.

A SURVEY OF POLICE AGENCIES

When qualitative research is used in an exploratory role its purpose is to enhance the understanding of a phenomenon so as to gain insight about the topic of the research and therefore to be able to make generalizations that will result in testable hypotheses that can be used for a subsequent and confirmatory quantitative analysis (Stebbins 2001). However, more broadly exploration in social science research may be defined as a comprehensive, orderly, and focused project designed to describe and understand social phenomena and thereby facilitate later data collection and analysis (Vogt and Johnson 2011). In that sense it is possible for the collection and analysis of quantitative data to be used to inform subsequent qualitative data collection and analysis. For the study on which this book is based we collected exploratory quantitative survey data from police agencies in the United States about local methamphetamine markets to inform our subsequent collection and analysis of qualitative data from individual and group interviews with people who in one way or another participate in those markets, and observations of places and social situations and settings that are in some way related to them.

Police officials and officers are neither the only nor arguably the best source of information about methamphetamine markets, even the markets in their own jurisdiction. And certainly their understanding and explanation of how those markets are organized and how they operate is only one of many. But for the exploratory purpose of our study at this stage we purposefully chose police agencies as the source of respondents for our survey. As noted earlier, the aim of the survey as the first of the three stages of our study was to collect data that would help us to determine where active meth markets were located and to learn something about similarities and differences in different places. The idea was to distinguish and locate different types of meth markets so we could focus the later phases of our study on understanding and explaining commonalities and dissimilarities. Recognizing that the knowledge and perspective of local police, like that of any other social actor, would be related to their social position and experience (Ryan et al. 1990; see also Berger and Luckmann 1966), we chose to start with police given that they do represent a common institution in all communities that have a responsibility for and vested interest in knowing where to locate illicit drug markets, knowing something about how those markets are organized and how they operate, and knowing something about their impact on the people and community in which they are located.

The National Public Safety Information Bureau annually publishes its National Directory of Law Enforcement Administrators database as a comprehensive listing of all law enforcement agencies across the country. In 2007 the database included 15,917 agencies, including municipal police departments and independent city sheriffs, county police and sheriff's departments, state police/highway patrol headquarters, and state criminal investigation headquarters. Using that listing as a sampling frame we assigned each agency to one of twenty-seven groups based on its location relative to the nine Organized Crime Drug Enforcement Task Force regions, as well as three levels of metropolitan or urbanicity status. Then we systematically selected a sample of 4,389 law enforcement agencies and sent each a questionnaire asking closed-ended questions about the extent of methamphetamine use and markets in their jurisdiction, the source of the drug, where it was sold, its relationship if any to local problems, and how the local market was organized and operated in terms of patterns of buying, selling, production, and use. The cover letter indicated that the questionnaire should be completed by the agency representative in their office with the greatest familiarity with narcotics investigations, particularly methamphetamine. Agencies could respond by mail, fax, or e-mail and follow-up calls were made as needed. A total of 1,367 agencies covering all fifty states responded.

The screening survey was never intended to produce a representative sample of agencies or communities that acknowledged having methamphetamine markets. Rather, the purpose was to provide data that could be used to identify different types of markets in different places to help us select places and people to contact for open-ended interviews and later site visits. Our goal was to learn where we could find active meth markets with particular characteristics and local people who were knowledgeable about those markets and would be willing to talk about them. Thus, instead of investing our resources in maximizing our response rate we devoted resources to helping us gain a wide-ranging overview of the national geographical and social landscape of methamphetamine markets and their similarities and variability.

From our survey we did learn something about what methamphetamine markets across America have in common. For example, of the 1,367 police agencies that had someone respond to our survey questions we learned that most often:

- buyers repeatedly use the same seller (94 percent of the respondents said yes)
- buyers and sellers of meth in their area knew each other (93 percent)
- meth in their area was sold in private homes (91 percent)
- meth sales involve cell phones (97 percent)
- the quality of meth changes regularly (72 percent)

In summary, we learned that—compared to other illicit retail drug markets, such as street corner crack cocaine markets—methamphetamine markets are personal, involving people who know each other transacting business in their homes. Our survey respondents also told us a few things that suggested to us how meth markets might vary. For example:

- people who work in drug markets have distinct roles (58 percent)
- local retail markets are well organized (55 percent)

- there is competition among sellers (52 percent)
- competition in meth markets is often violent (46 percent)
- meth dealers have clearly defined territories (21 percent)
- meth buyers buy in their own neighborhood (31 percent)

In these cases half or fewer of the respondents agreed with a statement. From these responses we were able to conclude that in some places methamphetamine markets are more or less organized and more or less competitive than others. These findings told us something about the commonalities and variability we should be looking for in the next phases of our study. More important for that purpose was what we learned from a cluster analysis of the survey data.

Statistically, a cluster analysis is an exploratory data analysis tool used to group objects into a taxonomy of meaningful categories (Tryon 1939). With our survey data we used a cluster analytic technique (Everitt et al. 2001; Romesburg 1990) to collapse the 1,367 police jurisdictions into meaningful categories that distinguished the type of market or markets and the mix of market types in the area. Our clusters were largely based on the responses to questions about the source of methamphetamine in the local area and how the respondents described the relative seriousness for public health, public safety, and the local economy of meth in the area. For 9 percent (121) of the areas in our sample of police jurisdictions we did not have sufficient data to include them in our analysis and respondents in about one-fifth of the areas reported no local meth markets (292, or 21 percent). This latter finding is consistent with available national statistics showing that methamphetamine use is not and has not been evenly distributed across the country (National Drug Intelligence Center 2005; National Institute of Justice 2003b; Office of National Drug Control Policy 2011b). Of the remaining 954 respondents (70 percent) that did report having active methamphetamine markets in their area, each reported one or more sources of the drug: local production, imported meth from Mexico or meth imported directly from another state but probably originally from Mexico. These places varied in the extent to which they reported local public health and safety problems associated with the local meth markets. Only 194 of the respondents reported a single source of meth in the area, and the remainder reported two or more sources. Overall, the primary distinction between communities with active methamphetamine markets was that some were dominated by local laboratory production and others by imported product, mostly from Mexico. In general, we found that methamphetamine markets were more common in some parts of the country than others, and that some areas with markets reportedly had widespread availability of meth from a variety of sources and a serious local problem while others had ongoing but limited market activity. Using our cluster analysis technique we determined that our most productive approach would be to select police agencies from each of the following types of areas: those primarily with local production "mom-and-pop" markets, those primarily with import markets, and those with a mix of both. We chose a total of fifty agencies for the next phase of the study, the in-depth telephone interviews with knowledgeable and interested narcotics police respondents.

THE TELEPHONE INTERVIEWS

The fifty police agencies with which we conducted telephone interviews were selected from areas with different types or mixes of types of methamphetamine markets and a high level of knowledge about those markets. In all cases officials had agreed through the survey they returned to participate and provided contact information for the person in the department considered most knowledgeable about local methamphetamine markets. The respondents were contacted and interviewed by telephone for at least one hour and sometimes as long as two, providing detailed information about what they know about the organization and operation of meth markets in their local area.

Initially we conceptualized methamphetamine markets as being organized and operating in specific locations in particular communities where methamphetamine transactions took place. From our surveys we began to see that local markets are also connected to the wider production and distribution of methamphetamine in the surrounding region and even the nation and possibly other nations, in particular but not only in the case of import markets. So when we began the interview phase of the study we saw it as an opportunity to learn more about the local markets and their connections beyond the local area in more depth with people knowledgeable about and involved in the local markets. Specifically, we interviewed narcotics police respondents who had personal responsibility for investigating those markets.

The in-depth or intensive interview is a well-established qualitative method of data collection and there is a considerable literature on how to conduct such interviews and on their value as a research technique (e.g., Brownstein 1983; DiCicco-Bloom and Crabtree 2006; Johnson 2002; Merton and Kendall 1946; Seidman 2006; Weiss 1975). Similarly, there is a research literature on the challenges of successful interviewing (e.g., Gorden 1956; Holloway and Jefferson 1997; Miller 1995; Rice 1929; Seidman 2006). Challenges may include getting people to talk to you, finding the right people to talk with, asking the right questions to elicit the relevant information, and getting respondents to be truthful and comprehensive given the subjective nature of the information they are providing.

To address the challenges of open-ended, intensive interviewing, particularly by telephone, we employed available sources of relevant data and various forms of contemporary technology. Interviews were conducted over the telephone, but in each case the respondent and interviewer were connected simultaneously by a web-based conferencing software program (WebEx) that allowed them to share written, graphic, and pictorial images. Most notably, using geocoded Google maps they could interactively share an image of a map of the area and region where the respondent was located.

Our plan from the beginning was to provide the telephone respondents with a map on which they could identify specific locations of local methamphetamine market transactions. To begin we gathered and organized publicly available, address-level meth laboratory seizure data from the DEA's National Clandestine Laboratory Register (NCLR, data available at http://www.justice.gov/dea/seizures/index.html). Although the NCLR is not a definitive listing of all methamphetamine labs in the United States, it is a comprehensive list of all known laboratories to which law enforcement has responded and as such is an exceptionally broad and detailed source of information for illicit drug activity. The observations in the register represent all locations where law enforcement found and documented chemicals or other materials that led them to believe there was an illicit drug laboratory at that address, though the register does not contain any information about the nature or scale of what they found. For each respondent we geocoded the addresses of all the methamphetamine seizures in their county and the surrounding counties using an online geocoding tool (MapAList; Create and Manage Maps of Address Lists available at http://mapalist.com/). Limiting the coding to their area was necessary as geocoding the entirety of the seizure data (for all fifty states spanning multiple years) made the maps unwieldy when the process was being tested. The resulting Google map was then shared with the respondent during the WebEx telephone interview or "meeting," during which both the respondent and the interviewer could manipulate and annotate the map while discussing events, settings, and experiences related to the local meth market or markets.

All of the interviews were recorded and stored on a secure hard drive. The text was transcribed and audio and maps with their markings remained available for listening and viewing on a computer. We treated the transcribed narratives, the audio of the actual interview, and the visuals of the maps as data. We found that respondents became more engaged during the interview and used geographical markers to recall comprehensive information and detail about not only the location but also the operation and organization of local markets. The approach we used enhanced the quality of the data from our in-depth interviews by helping us to establish rapport between the interviewer and respondent and helping respondents to recall the details of events and circumstances and to better explain them.

Our approach facilitated the establishment of rapport with our police respondents in two ways. First, in each case we spent time prior to the interview working with the respondent to set up the WebEx connection. Then we provided the respondent with training on how to use WebEx; share the desktop; navigate the map; zoom in and out; use the Google facilities including the hybrid, satellite, and pole cam features; and use the pointer/marker. In effect the interviews became "virtual ride-alongs" for the interviewers with the police respondents. Respondents acknowledged the way the technological tools we were using gave them the ability to talk about regional differences while at the same time seeing an image of the actual places where particular activities or crimes had occurred. For example, together the interviewer and respondent could view specific locations or intersections or buildings and could recognize and appreciate the significance and importance of highways connecting interstate transit routes and mountains isolating or at least limiting expansion of some meth markets.

Our approach, and in particular the use of the geocoded Google maps, was also helpful in assisting respondents to recall details about the events being discussed. The maps and the markings showing where and when specific seizures had taken place, some of which they had personally been involved in, helped respondents to recall specific details about those events and to report them to the interviewer. One feature that made an important difference was the inclusion of colored balloons each representing a particular local methamphetamine laboratory or crime scene event by year on the maps being presented to the respondent through the computer connection. As noted earlier, these specific locations were extracted from the DEA NCLR database showing sites of meth seizures over five years. Each was coded so that when the interviewer or respondent moved the computer cursor over the balloon it showed the exact address and date of the seizure.

Each interview began with a series of questions to assess the nature of local drug markets, the health and safety impacts on the local community, and the experience of the respondent in narcotics enforcement. Once these questions were answered, respondents were given access to their local map and asked to tell us what they could about the points indicated by the seizure data in their jurisdiction and more broadly to use the annotation tool to show and describe drug markets and other areas of drug activity in their area. In some areas the seizure points were a remarkably good proxy for methamphetamine activity, and respondents had little difficulty delineating methamphetamine and other drug activity on the map. Whether or not this was the case, however, discussing the geography of markets invariably elicited the narrative experience of local narcotics enforcement and made them much more forthcoming in their responses. After the mapping section of the interview had concluded, the respondent was asked a series of follow-up questions based on our original survey questions about the organization and operation of methamphetamine markets.

The primary purpose of the telephone interviews was to learn about the organization and operation of local methamphetamine markets from people who knew about their local markets from personal experience, particularly from law enforcement people who had personal responsibility for controlling the markets in their community. A secondary purpose of the interviews was to help us to identify communities or regions to conduct site visits where we could make observations and conduct open-ended, in-person interviews not only with police but also with other market participants including drug treatment and family service providers, prevention program workers, meth users, and meth dealers, among others. The site visits were the third and final phase of our study.

THE SITE VISITS

Based on our survey and interview findings we selected five regions within the United States for in-depth data collection and analysis and identified communities within those regions to visit. We chose to visit regions rather than specific cities or towns because the analyses of our survey and interview data showed us that different areas have different types and mixes of types of markets, notably some having mostly local production markets while others have mostly product imported from elsewhere and others have both. But more importantly our analyses also demonstrated to us that individual markets located in particular places inexorably are connected to one another as part of a wider network of producers, distributors, and even other local markets of consumers extending beyond geographical or social boundaries. Then, once we selected regions naturally it helped to be able to arrange our visits through local people we already knew and who already knew us, specifically the narcotics police we had interviewed over the telephone and the police officers and officials who had participated in our survey.

For the most part the regions and communities within those regions that we selected were chosen on the basis of what we had learned from the survey and interview data about the organization and operation of local methamphetamine markets and their impact on the people who lived and worked there. A secondary yet perhaps equally important selection criterion was the extent to which we would have access and be able to talk to a mix of different people who had experienced the local meth market or markets in a variety of ways. That is, for the site visit phase of the research we were ready to go beyond what law enforcement people had told us about methamphetamine markets in their area from their significant but singular perspective. We wanted and needed to talk to people who had different relationships and connections to the markets and to see the markets through different sets of eyes.

As noted earlier, we started with the police because law enforcement officials and officers, especially narcotics police, have a responsibility to maintain order and to prevent and investigate crime related to drug use and markets, so they do have a special and vested interest in knowing how those markets are organized and how they operate. That proved to be particularly valuable in the first two stages of our research, when our goal was to get a lay of the land. For the third stage our objective shifted to understanding and being able to explain different types of places with different types of methamphetamine markets from the perspective of the people who participate in those markets in different ways. The police we had gotten to know and who had gotten to know us and to trust us were able to help us accomplish that objective. The local law enforcement people with whom we had established relationships through the survey and the interviews served as our hosts and guides, introducing us to other people in their community, including meth users and dealers and those who worked with local methamphetamine users and their families.

Over the course of about one year we visited five regions of the United States where we knew there to be particular types or mixes of types of active methamphetamine markets and people who would be interested in talking about them. Although official data on methamphetamine sales and use are not available, there are statistics derived from surrogate measures. For example, the Arrestee Drug Abuse Monitoring program sponsored by the National Institute of Justice, the research arm of the U.S. Department of Justice, for a period of years annually collected interview data and tested urine samples for a variety of illicit drugs from tens of thousands of arrestees in thirty-five counties within forty-eight hours of arrest. Results of the urine testing in the year 2000 showed that the highest rates of methamphetamine use among arrestees was found in cities and counties in western states including Honolulu (36 percent), Sacramento (29 percent), San Diego (26 percent), Portland (21 percent), Spokane (20 percent), Phoenix (19 percent), and Las Vegas (18 percent). In many eastern and midwestern counties the rates of methamphetamine use among tested arrestees was at or close to zero, as in Chicago, Detroit, Fort Lauderdale, Miami, New York, and Philadelphia (National Institute of Justice 2003a). More recently, in 2010 in a smaller version of Arrestee Drug Abuse Monitoring sponsored by the Office of National Drug Control Policy (ONDCP) in ten counties, more than 30 percent of sampled arrestees tested positive for methamphetamine in Sacramento and almost 20 percent in Portland, while again the proportion remained at less than 1 percent in midwestern and eastern cities including Chicago, New York, and Atlanta (Office of National Drug Control Policy 2011b).

Given that historically available records showed that methamphetamine in America was largely a western phenomenon, naturally we were interested in visiting places in western regions of the country. In each region we flew to a major city and then drove from place to place throughout the area. In the Pacific Northwest we visited the cities and surrounding suburbs in Seattle, Washington, and Portland, Oregon. Then we traveled south and visited other places in Oregon including Salem, Eugene, and Medford. Oregon was particularly interesting because state legislation had closed down local production and almost all the methamphetamine in the area was imported from Mexico. We also visited the Southwest, stopping in and around Las Vegas and Reno in Nevada and Phoenix and Yuma in Arizona. Given its proximity to the Mexican border, in the Southwest most of the methamphetamine markets similarly were supplied by imported product trafficked to the area from Mexico, or sometimes produced by Mexican manufacturing organizations in California.

Although available statistics suggested that most of the methamphetamine was being used and marketed in the West, our survey and interview data suggested that methamphetamine was being used in other parts of the country as well. As a result we decided to visit particular regions where statistics had not shown high levels of methamphetamine use but our respondents had told us otherwise. One place that appeared to be particularly interesting for learning about methamphetamine markets was the Southeast. In the Southeast we started near the city of Atlanta, Georgia, and worked our way through surrounding suburban and rural towns and villages. This was an area with a quiet history of meth production in local mom-and-pop labs that had become a hub for the distribution of methamphetamine produced in Mexico all up and down the East Coast. More than most other illicit drugs methamphetamine has been popular in rural areas, so in the Middle Atlantic we worked our way from Galax in rural southern Virginia near the North Carolina border through Blue Ridge Mountain towns such as Staunton and Marion all the way up into Maryland and finally

Washington, DC. Methamphetamine markets especially in the Midwest and particularly in rural areas appear to have remained true to an old tradition of homegrown production and Mexican importers have not been able to establish a base for distribution in the area. Our visits to cities, towns, and rural communities in the Midwest included St. Louis, Missouri, Carbondale, Illinois, Evansville, Indiana, Jacksonville, Illinois, and Henderson, Kentucky.

Ultimately we visited five regions of the country where we knew there to be active methamphetamine markets. We spent a week or more in each region and in total visited about twenty-eight cities and towns and the surrounding area. We spoke individually or in groups with local police, with representatives of intergovernmental drug task forces, government officials, drug treatment providers, drug prevention program workers, family service providers, methamphetamine dealers and cooks, methamphetamine users, and almost anyone else who had something to say and would talk with us (even occasionally people like taxicab drivers). The interviews mostly took place in offices or community centers, but there were other locations, including one time in a jail cell. We asked all of the people we interviewed some basic questions about the area and the local markets and marketing, but the interviews were always conversational following questions that had been left unanswered after we studied what we learned from the survey and telephone interview data. All questions were open ended, and all interviews were taped and transcribed. More often than not there were two or more interviewers working together so later we could compare notes and compare our interpretations of what we heard. Except in the case of methamphetamine users and dealers, who were interviewed by themselves, there was usually more than one person being interviewed at the same time. In one case we interviewed a roomful of people who worked with families whose lives had been disrupted by methamphetamine use and marketing among one or more family members. In another case we sat in a room with a police official, a police officer, an emergency room doctor, a drug prevention program worker, and a television news reporter. No interview lasted less than one hour, but many started out being scheduled for one hour and ended up lasting two or three. Sometimes when the interview was taking place in an office one person would leave after a while and another would join us.

Alone or with a guide we walked or drove through areas known to have meth users and dealers or to be a place where methamphetamine transactions occurred. By invitation we attended community events where local citizens talked about personal and community issues and problems related to local methamphetamine use and markets. While visiting Yuma, Arizona, we had the opportunity to tour a few miles of the border with Mexico near San Luis guided by a member of the U.S. Border Patrol. We were driven along the border fences and river, learned how people are trained to bring drugs across the border and where and how they do it, drove through neighborhoods where people who deliver methamphetamine and other drugs from Mexico stored the product when they arrived in the United States, and stopped to watch the activity at a legal border crossing.

References

Adler, Patricia. 1993. Wheeling and Dealing: An Ethnography of an Upper-Level Drug Dealing and Smuggling Community. New York: Columbia University Press.

Andrews, P. W. S. 1949. Manufacturing Business. London: Macmillan.

Beith, Malcolm. 2010. The Last Narco—Inside the Hunt for El Chapo, the World's Most Wanted Drug Lord. New York: Grove Press.

Bellair, Paul E., and Thomas L. McNulty. 2009. "Gang Membership, Drug Selling, and Violence in Neighborhood Context." Justice Quarterly 26:644–669.

Berg, Mark T., and Andres F. Rengifo. 2009. "Rethinking Community Organization and Robbery: Considering Illicit Market Dynamics." Justice Quarterly 26:211–237.

Berger, Peter L. 1963. Invitation to Sociology: A Humanistic Perspective. Garden City, NY: Doubleday & Co.

Berger, Peter L., Brigitte Berger, and Robert Binks. 1975. Sociology—A Biographical Approach. New York: Basic Books.

Berger , Peter L., and Thomas Luckmann. 1966. The Social Construction of Reality—A Treatise in the Sociology of Knowledge. Garden City, NY: Doubleday & Co.

Blumer, Herbert. 1969. Symbolic Interaction—Perspective and Method. Englewood Cliffs, NJ: Prentice-Hall.

Bogdan, Robert, and Steven J. Taylor. 1975. Introduction to Qualitative Research Methods—A Phenomenological Approach to the Social Sciences. New York: John Wiley & Sons.

Bourgois, Philippe. 1995. In Search of Respect—Selling Crack in El Barrio. New York: Cambridge University Press.

Brouwer, Kimberly C., Patricia Case, Rebeca Ramos, Carlos Magis-Rodríguez, Jesus Bucardo, Thomas L. Patterson, and Steffanie A. Strathdee. 2006. "Trends in Production, Trafficking, and Consumption of Methamphetamine and Cocaine in Mexico." Substance Use and Misuse 41:707–727.

Brownstein, Henry H. 1983. "The Adequacy of Intensive Interview Data: Preliminary Suggestions for the Measurement of Validity." Humanity and Society 7:301–320.

———. 2000a. "Drug Distribution and Sales as a Work System." In Encyclopedia of Criminology and Deviant Behavior, Volume 4: Self Destructive Behavior and Disvalued Identity, edited by Charles E. Faupel and Paul M. Roman, 224–227. Philadelphia: Taylor and Francis.

———. 2000b. The Social Reality of Violence and Violent Crime. Boston: Allyn and Bacon.

Brownstein, Henry H., Susan M. Crimmins, and Barry J. Spunt. 2000. "A Conceptual Framework for Operationalizing the Relationship between Violence and Drug Market Stability." Contemporary Drug Problems 27:867–890.

Brownstein, Henry H., Timothy M. Mulcahy, Johannes Fernandes-Huessy, Bruce G. Taylor, and Daniel Woods. 2012a. "The Organization and Operation of Illicit Retail Methamphetamine Markets." Criminal Justice Policy Review 23:67–89.

Brownstein, Henry H., Timothy M. Mulcahy, Bruce G. Taylor, Johannes Fernandes-Huessy, and Carol Hafford. 2012b. "Home Cooking: Marketing Meth." Contexts 11:30–35.

Brownstein, Henry H., and Bruce G. Taylor. 2007. "Measuring the Stability of Illicit Drug Markets: Why Does It Matter?" Drug and Alcohol Dependence 90:52–60.

Campion, Emily. 2013. "As Meth-Making Expands, Some Ask, Where Is It Safe?" jconline.com. Accessed July 16, 2013. http://www.jconline.com/article/20130406/NEWS03/304060020/.

Caulkins, Jonathan P. 2005. "Price and Purity Analysis for Illicit Drugs: Data and Conceptual Issues." Heinz Research Paper 25. http://repository.cmu.edu/heinzworks/25.

Caulkins, Jonathan P. and Peter Reuter. 1997. "Setting Goals for Drug Policy: Harm Reduction or Use Reduction?" Addiction 92:1143–1150.

———. 1998. "What Price Data Tell Us about Drug Markets." Journal of Drug Issues 28:593–612.

———. 2004. "Illicit Drug Markets and Economic Irregularities." Socio-Economic Planning Sciences 40:1–14.

———. 2010. "How Drug Enforcement Affects Drug Prices." Crime and Justice 39:213–271.

City of Galax, Virginia. 2013. "Galax, Virginia." Accessed April 21, 2013. http://www.city-data.com/city/Galax-Virginia.html#ixzz289s2xkCh.

City of Holdrege, Nebraska. 2013. "Holdrege Facts and Statistics." Accessed June 30, 2013. http://www.cityofholdrege.org/holdrege_info.asp?pid=4.

City of Saint Louis, Missouri. "Government Page." Accessed November 13, 2013. https://stlouis-mo.gov/.

City of Tacoma, Washington. 2013. "Tacoma: Economy." Accessed July 2, 2013. http://www.city-data.com/us-cities/The-West/Tacoma-Economy.html.

Cohen, Judith B., Alice Dickow, Kathryn Horner, Joan E. Zweben, Joseph Balabis, Denna Vandersloot, and Chris Reiber. 2003. "Abuse and Violence History of Men and Women in Treatment for Methamphetamine Dependence." American Journal on Addictions 12:377–385.

Creswell, John W., and Vicki L. Plano Clark. 2011. Designing and Conducting Mixed Methods Research. 2nd ed. Thousand Oaks, CA: Sage.

Curtis, Richard, Samuel R. Friedman, Alan Neaigus, Benny Jose, Marjorie Goldstein, and Gilbert Ildefonso. 1995. "Street-Level Drug Markets: Network Structure and HIV Risk." Social Networks 17: 229–249.

Curtis, Ric, and Travis Wendel. 2000. "Toward the Development of a Typology of Illegal Drug Markets." Crime Prevention Studies 11:121–152.

————. 2002. Final Report: Drug Markets on the Lower East Side of Manhattan. Washington, DC: National Institute of Justice.

Darke, Shane, Sharlene Kaye, Rebecca McKetin, and Johan Duflou. 2008. "Major Physical and Psychological Harms of Methamphetamine Use." Drug and Alcohol Review 27:253–262.

Dembo, Richard, Patrick Hughes, Lisa Jackson, and Thomas Mieczkowski. 1993. "Crack Cocaine Dealing by Adolescents in Two Public Housing Projects: A Pilot Study." Human Organization 52:89–96.

Dembo, Richard, Linda Williams, Werner Wothke, James Schmeidler, Alan Getreu, Estrillita Berry, Eric D. Wish, and Candice Christensen. 1990. "The Relationship between Cocaine Use, Drug Sales, and Other Delinquency among a Cohort of High Risk Youths over Time." In Drugs and Violence: Causes, Correlates, and Consequences, edited by Mario De La Rosa, Elizabeth Y. Lambert, and Bernard Gropper, 112–135. NIDA Research Monograph No. 103. Rockville, MD: National Institute on Drug Abuse.

Denzin, Norman K., and Yvonna S. Lincoln. 2011. "Introduction—The Discipline and Practice of Qualitative Research." In Handbook of Qualitative Research, 4th ed., edited by Norman K. Denzin and Yvonna S. Lincoln, 1–20. Thousand Oaks, CA: Sage.

Desroches, Frederick. 2007. "Research on Upper-Level Drug Trafficking: A Review." Journal of Drug Issues 37:827–844.

De Vito, Michael J., and G. C. Wagner. 1989. "Methamphetamine-Induced Neuronal Damage: A Possible Role for Free Radicals." Neuropharmacology 28:1145–1150.

DiCicco-Bloom, Barbara, and Benjamin F. Crabtree. 2006. "The Qualitative Research Interview." Medical Education 40:314–321.

Duffy, Mary E. 1987. "Methodological Triangulation: A Vehicle for Merging Quantitative and Qualitative Research Methods." Journal of Nursing Scholarship 19:130–133.

Durkheim, Émile. 1938. The Rules of Sociological Method. 8th ed. Translated by Sarah A. Solovay and John H. Mueller. Edited by George E. G. Catlin. New York: Free Press.

Eck, John E. 1995. "A General Model of the Geography of Illicit Retail Market Places." In Crime and Place: Crime Prevention Studies, edited by John E. Eck and David Weisburd, 168–193. Monsey, NY: Criminal Justice Press.

Eck, John E., and Jeffrey S. Gersh. 2000. "Drug Trafficking as a Cottage Industry." Crime Prevention Studies 11:241–271.

Everitt, Brian S., Sabine Landau, Morven Leese, and Daniel Stahl. 2001. Cluster Analysis. 4th ed. London: Edward Arnold.

Fagan, Jeffrey. 1989. "The Social Organization of Drug Use and Drug Dealing among Urban Gangs." Criminology 27:633–669.

Fagan, Jeffrey, and Ko-lin Chin. 1990. "Violence as Regulation and Social Control in the Distribution of Crack." In Drugs and Violence: Causes, Correlates, and Consequences, edited by Mario De La Rosa, Elizabeth Y. Lambert, and Bernard Gropper, 8–43. NIDA Research Monograph No. 103. Rockville, MD: National Institute on Drug Abuse.

Faules, Don. 1982. "The Use of Multi-Methods in the Organizational Setting." Western Journal of Speech Communication 46:150–161.

Federal Advisory Committee. 2000. Final Report. Washington, DC: Methamphetamine Interagency Task Force.

Federal Bureau of Investigation. 2011. Crime in the United States, 2010. Washington, DC: U.S. Department of Justice.

Fligstein, Neil, and Luke Dauter. 2007. "The Sociology of Markets." Annual Review of Sociology 33:105–128.

Fourcade, Marion. 2007. "Theories of Markets and Theories of Society." American Behavioral Scientist 50:1015–1034.

Fries, Arthur, Robert W. Anthony, Andrew Cseko Jr., Carl C. Gaither, and Eric Schulman. 2008. Technical Report for the Price and Purity of Illicit Drugs: 1981–2007. IDA Paper P-4370. Alexandria, VA: Institute for Defense Analysis.

Funk, Brian. 2006. "The Story of Galax." Gazette. Galax, VA: Landmark Community Newspapers.

Geertz, Clifford. 1973. The Interpretation of Cultures. New York: Basic Books.

Glaser, Barney, and Anselm L. Strauss. 1967. The Discovery of Grounded Theory—Strategies for Qualitative Research. Chicago: Aldine-Atherton.

Goldstein, Paul J., Henry H. Brownstein, and Patrick J. Ryan. 1992. "Drug-Related Homicide in New York: 1984 and 1988." Crime and Delinquency 38:459–476.

Goldstein, Paul J., Henry H. Brownstein, Patrick J. Ryan, and Patricia A. Bellucci. 1989. "Crack and Homicide in New York City: A Conceptually Based Event Analysis." Contemporary Drug Problems 13:651–687.

Gonzales, Rachel, Larissa Mooney, and Richard A. Rawson. 2010. "The Methamphetamine Problem in the United States." Annual Review of Public Health 31:385–398.

Gorden, Raymond L. 1956. "Dimensions of the Depth Interview." American Journal of Sociology 62:158–164.

Gordon, Milton M. 1964. Assimilation in American Life: The Role of Race, Religion, and National Origins. New York: Oxford University Press.

Harocopos, Alex, and Mike Hough. 2006. Drug Dealing in Open-Air Markets. Problem-Oriented Guides for Police Problem-Specific Guides Series, No. 31. Washington, DC: Community Oriented Policing Services, U.S. Department of Justice.

Herz, Denise C. 2000. Drugs in the Heartland: Methamphetamine Use in Rural Nebraska. Washington, DC: U.S. Department of Justice, Office of Justice Programs, National Institute of Justice.

Holloway, Wendy, and Tony Jefferson. 1997. "Eliciting Narrative through the In-Depth Interview." Qualitative Inquiry 3:53–70.

Hughes, Patrick H. 1977. Behind the Wall of Respect: Community Experiments in Heroin Addiction Control. Chicago: University of Chicago Press.

Hughes, Patrick H., Gail A. Crawford, Noel W. Barker, Suzanne Schumann, and Jerome H. Jaffe. 1971. "The Social Structure of a Heroin Copping Community." American Journal of Psychiatry 128:551–558.

Hunt, Dana. 2004. "Characterizing Drug Markets: A Comparison of Crack and Methamphetamine Markets." Presented at a NIDA workshop, Drug Abuse: A Workshop on Behavioral and Economic Research. Bethesda, MD.

Hunt, Dana, Sarah Kuck, and Linda Truitt. 2005. Methamphetamine Use: Lessons Learned. Report submitted to the National Institute of Justice. Cambridge, MA: Abt Associates.

Jacobs, Bruce A. 1999. Dealing Crack—The Social World of Streetcorner Selling. Boston: Northeastern University Press.

Jacques, Scott. 2010. "The Necessary Conditions for Retaliation: Toward a Theory of Non-Violent and Violent Forms in Drug Markets." Justice Quarterly 27:186–205.

Jick, Todd D. 1979. "Mixing Qualitative and Quantitative Methods: Triangulation in Action." Administrative Science Quarterly 4:602–611.

Johnson, Bruce D., Paul J. Goldstein, Edward Preble, James Schmeidler, Douglas S. Lipton, Barry Spunt, and Thomas Miller. 1985. Taking Care of Business: The Economics of Crime by Heroin Abusers. Lexington, MA: Lexington Books.

Johnson, Bruce D., Ansley Hamid, and Harry Sanabria. 1992. "Emerging Models of Crack Distribution." In Drugs, Crime, and Social Policy: Research, Issues, and Concerns, edited by Thomas Mieczkowski, 56–78. Boston: Allyn and Bacon.

Johnson, John M. "In-Depth Interviewing." 2002. In Handbook of Interview Research: Context and Method, edited by Jaber F. Gubrium and James A. Holstein, 103–120. Thousand Oaks, CA: Sage.

Johnson, R. Burke, and Anthony J. Onwuegbuzie. 2004. "Mixed Methods Research: A Research Paradigm Whose Time Has Come." Educational Researcher 33:14–26.

Kaplan, Abraham. 1964. The Conduct of Inquiry: Methodology for Behavioral Science. San Francisco: Chandler.

Kaye, Sharlene, Rebecca McKetin, Johan Duflou, and Shane Darke. 2007. "Methamphetamine and Cardiovascular Pathology: A Review of the Evidence." Addiction 102:1204–1211.

Kerr, Thomas, Will Small, and Evan Wood. 2005. "The Public Health and Social Impacts of Drug Market Enforcement: A Review of the Evidence." International Journal of Drug Policy 16:210–220.

Kleiman, Mark A. R. 1992. Against Excess: Drug Policy for Results. New York: Basic Books.

Kleiman, Mark A. R., Jonathan P. Caulkins, and Angela Hawken. 2011. Drugs and Drug Policy—What Everyone Needs to Know. New York: Oxford University Press.

Kluckhohn, Clyde. 1944. Mirror for Man: A Survey of Human Behavior and Social Attitudes. New York: McGraw Hill.

Kotkin, Joel. 2004. "Top 25 Cities for Doing Business in America." Inc., March 1. http://www.inc.com/magazine/20040301/top25_pagen_2.html.

Kroeber, A. L., and Clyde Kluckhohn. 1952. Culture: A Critical Review of Concepts and Definitions. New York: Random House.

Kunkin, Art. 1965. "Interview with Allen Ginsberg." Los Angeles Free Press, December.

Langton, Jerry. 2012. Gangland: The Rise of the Mexican Drug Cartels from El Paso to Vancouver. Mississauga, Ontario: John Wiley and Sons Canada.

Lazarsfeld, Paul Felix and Morris Rosenberg. 1955. The Language of Social Research: A Reader in the Methodology of Social Research. Edited by Morris Rosenberg. New York: Free Press.

Levitt, Steven D., and Sudhir Alladi Venkatesh. 2000. "An Economic Analysis of a Drug-Selling Gang's Finances." Quarterly Journal of Economics 115:755–789.

Lu, Max, and Jessica Burnum. 2008. "Spatial Patterns of Clandestine Methamphetamine Labs in Colorado Springs, Colorado." In Geography and Drug Addiction, edited by Yonette F. Thomas, Douglas Richardson, and Ivan Cheung, 193–208. New York: Springer.

May, Tiggey, and Mike Hough. 2004. "Drug Markets and Distribution Systems." Addiction Research and Theory 12:549–563.

Maher, Lisa. 2005. Sexed Work: Gender, Race, and Resistance in a Brooklyn Drug Market. New York: Oxford University Press.

Martínez, Ramiro, Jr., Richard Rosenfeld, and Dennis Mares. 2011. "Social Disorganization, Drug Market Activity, and Neighborhood Violent Crime." Urban Affairs Review 43:846–874.

McBride, Duane C., Yvonne M. Terry-McElrath, Jamie F. Chriqui, Jean C. O'Connor, Curtis J. VanderWaal, and Karen L. Mattson. 2011. "State Methamphetamine Precursor Policies and Changes in Small Toxic Lab Methamphetamine." Journal of Drug Issues (Fall): 253–282.

McBride, Duane C., Curtis J. VanderWaal, and Yvonne M. Terry-McElrath. 2003. "The Drugs-Crime Wars: Past, Present, and Future Directions in Theory, Policy, and Program Interventions." In Toward a Drugs and Crime Research Agenda for the 21st Century, 97–161. National Institute of Justice Special Report. Washington, DC: U.S. Department of Justice.

McKetin, Rebecca, Jennifer McLaren, and Erin Kelly. 2005. The Sydney Methamphetamine Market: Patterns of Supply, Use, Personal Harms and Social Consequences. Mongraph Series No. 13. National Drug Law Enforcement Research Fund. Sydney, Australia: National Alcohol and Drug Research Centre.

Mead, George Herbert. 1964. On Social Psychology. Chicago: University of Chicago Press.

Merton, Robert K. 1968. Social Theory and Social Structure. New York: Free Press.

Merton, Robert K., and Patricia L. Kendall. 1946. "The Focused Interview." American Journal of Sociology 51:541–555.

Mieczkowski, Thomas. 1990. "Crack Distribution in Detroit." Contemporary Drug Problems 17:9–29.

———. 1992. "Crack Dealing on the Street—The Crew System and the Crack House." Justice Quarterly 9:151–163.

Miller, Carol. 1995. "In-Depth Interviewing by Telephone: Some Practical Considerations." Evaluation and Research in Education 9:29–38.

Morgan, David L. 1998. "Practical Strategies for Combining Qualitative and Quantitative Methods: Applications to Health Research." Qualitative Health Research 8:362–376.

Murphy, Sheigla, Paloma Sales, Micheline Duterte, and Camille Jacinto. 2005. A Qualitative Study of Ecstasy Sellers in the San Francisco Bay Area. Document 209267. Report to the National Institute of Justice. Washington, DC: U.S. Department of Justice.

National Academy of Sciences. 2013a. "Mission." Accessed July 16, 2013. http://www.nasonline.org/about-nas/mission/.

National Academy of Sciences. 2013b. "Welcome to the National Research Council." Accessed July 16, 2013. http://www.nas.edu/nrc/index.html.

National Climatic Data Center. 2013. "Extremes in U.S. Climate." Accessed June 30, 2013 http://www.ncdc.noaa.gov/extremes/extreme-us-climates.php#SUN-CLOUD.

National Drug Intelligence Center. 2005. Methamphetamine Drug Threat Assessment. No. 2005-Q0317–009. Washington, DC: U.S. Department of Justice.

———. 2010. National Drug Threat Assessment 2010. No. 2010-Q0317–001. Washington, DC: U.S. Department of Justice.

———. 2011. National Drug Threat Assessment 2011. No. 2011-Q0317–001. Washington, DC: U.S. Department of Justice.

———. 2013. "About NDIC." Accessed July 16, 2013. http://www.justice.gov/archive/ndic/about.htm.

National Institute on Drug Abuse. 2013. "DrugFacts: Methamphetamine." Accessed July 16, 2013. http://www.drugabuse.gov/publications/drugfacts/methamphetamine.

National Institute of Justice. 1999. Meth Matters: Report on Methamphetamine Users in Five Western Cities. NCJ 176331. Washington, DC: U.S. Department of Justice.

———. 2003a. Toward a Drugs and Crime Research Agenda for the 21st Century. Special Report. Washington, DC: U.S. Department of Justice.

———. 2003b. Annual Report 2000—Arrestee Drug Abuse Monitoring. Washington, DC: National Institute of Justice, US Department of Justice.

National Institute on Drug Abuse. 2010. Methamphetamine. NIDA InfoFacts. Rockville, MD: U.S. Department of Health and Human Services. Accessed October 17, 2012. http://drugabuse.gov/publications/drugfacts/methamphetamine.

National Research Council. 2001. Informing America's Policy on Illegal Drugs: What We Don't Know Keeps Hurting Us. Commission on Behavioral and Social Sciences and Education. Washington, DC: National Academy Press.

———. 2010. Understanding the Demand for Illegal Drugs. Committee on Law and Justice. Washington, DC: National Academy Press.

Neale, Alice, Suzanne Abraham, and Janice Russell. 2009. "'Ice' Use and Eating Disorders: A Report of Three Cases." International Journal of Eating Disorders 42:188–191.

Nightingale, John. 1978. "On the Definition of 'Industry' and 'Market.'" Journal of Industrial Economics 27:31–40.

Office of the Inspector General. 2010. Review of the Drug Enforcement Administration's El Paso Intelligence Center. I-2010–005. Washington, DC: U.S. Department of Justice.

Office of National Drug Control Policy. 2011a. National Drug Control Strategy. Washington, DC: The White House.

———. 2011b. ADAM II. 2010 Annual Report. Arrestee Drug Abuse Monitoring Program II. Washington, DC: Office of National Drug Control Policy.

———. 2013. "About ONDCP." Accessed July 16, 2013. http://www.whitehouse.gov/ondcp/about.

Ousey, Graham C., and Matthew R. Lee. 2007. "Homicide Trends and Illicit Drug Markets: Exploring Differences across Time." Justice Quarterly 24:48–79.

Parsons, Talcott. 1956a. "Suggestions for a Sociological Approach to the Theory of Organizations, I." Administrative Science Quarterly 1:63–85.

————. 1956b. "Suggestions for a Sociological Approach to the Theory of Organizations, II." Administrative Science Quarterly 1:225–239.

Radcliffe-Brown, A. R. 1952. Structure and Function in Primitive Society. New York: Free Press.

Ragin, Charles C., and Lisa M. Amoroso. 2011. Constructing Social Research—The Unity and Diversity of Method. 2nd ed. Newbury Park, CA: Pine Forge Press.

Reuter, Peter, and Victoria Greenfield. 2001. "Measuring Global Drug Markets." World Economics 2:159–173.

Reuter, Peter, and John Haaga. 1989. The Organization of High Level Drug Markets: An Exploratory Study. Santa Monica: RAND.

Reuter, Peter, Robert MacCoun, and Patrick Murphy. 1990. Money from Crime: A Study of the Economics of Drug Dealing in Washington, DC. Santa Monica, CA: Drug Policy Research Center, RAND.

Rice, Stuart A. 1929. "Contagious Bias in the Interview." American Journal of Sociology 35:420–423.

Rhodes, William, Mary Layne, Patrick Johnston, and Lynne Hozik. 2000. What America's Users Spend on Illegal Drugs 1988–1998. Washington, DC: Office of National Drug Control Policy.

Ritter, Alison. 2006. "Studying Illicit Drug Markets: Disciplinary Contributions." International Journal of Drug Policy 17:453–463.

Romesburg, H. Charles. 1990. Cluster Analysis for Researchers. Malabar, FL: Krieger Publishing.

Ryan, Patrick J., Paul J. Goldstein, Henry H. Brownstein, and Patricia A. Bellucci. 1990. "Who's Right: Different Outcomes When Police and Scientists View the Same Set of Homicide Events." In Drugs and Violence: Causes, Correlates, and Consequences, edited by Mario De La Rosa, Elizabeth Y. Lambert, and Bernard Gropper, 239–64. National Institute on Drug Abuse Research Monograph 103. Rockville, MD: U.S. Department of Health and Human Services.

Salter, Jim. 2012. "The Big Story—AP Impact: Cartels Flood US with Cheap Meth." Associated Press, October 11. Accessed October 19, 2012. http://bigstory.ap.org/article/ap-impact-cartels-flood-us-cheap-meth.

Saner, Hilary, Robert J. MacCoun, and Peter Reuter. 1995. "On the Ubiquity of Drug Selling among Youthful Offenders in Washington, D.C., 1985–1991: Age, Period, or Cohort Effect?" Journal of Quantitative Criminology 11:337–362.

Scheck, Justin. 2010. "Meth Labs Make Return to U.S." Wall Street Journal, December 4. Accessed July 16, 2013. http://online.wsj.com/article/SB10001424052748703350104575653110796718070.html.

————. 2012. "Business Plan Remakes Meth Market." Wall Street Journal, September 13. Accessed July 16, 2013. http://online.wsj.com/article/SB10000872396390444772804577624090953289960.html.

Schutz, Alfred. 1954. "Concept and Theory Formation in the Social Sciences." Journal of Philosophy 51:257–73.

Scott, Jacques. 2010. "The Necessary Conditions for Retaliation: Toward a Theory of Non-Violent and Violent Forms in Drug Markets." Justice Quarterly 27:186–205.

Scott, Jacques, and Richard Wright. 2008. "The Relevance of Peace to Studies of Drug Market Violence." Criminology 46:221–253.

Seidman, Irving. 2006. Interviewing as Qualitative Research: A Guide for Researchers in Education and the Social Sciences. New York: Teachers College Press.

Shukla, Rashi K., Jordan L. Crump, and Emelia S. Chrisco. 2012. "An Evolving Problem: Methamphetamine Production and Trafficking in the United States." International Journal of Drug Addiction 23, no. 6 (November): 426–435.

Skolnick, Jerome H., Theodore Correl, Elizabeth Navarro, and Robert Rabb. 1990. "The Social Structure of Street Drug Dealing." American Journal of Police 9:1–42.

Small, Mario Luis. 2011. "How to Conduct a Mixed Methods Study: Recent Trends in a Rapidly Growing Literature." Annual Review of Sociology 37:57–86.

Smith, David E., Gantt P. Galloway, and Richard B. Seymour. 1997. "Methamphetamine Abuse, Violence, and Appropriate Treatment." Valparaiso University Law Review 31, no. 2: 661–667.

Sommers, Ira, Deborah Baskin, and Arielle Baskin-Sommers. 2006. "Methamphetamine Use among Young Adults: Health and Social Consequences." Addictive Behaviors 31:1469–1476.

Sonsalla, Patricia K., William J. Nicklas, and Richard E. Heikkila. 1989. "Role for Excitatory Amino Acids in Methamphetamine-Induced Nigrostriatal Dopaminergic Toxicity." Science 243, no. 4889:243–398.

Spergel, Irving. 1961. "An Exploratory Research in Delinquent Subcultures." Social Service Review 35:33–47.

Springfield News-Leader staff. 2007. "'Nazi Dope': Meth Reinvented in the Ozarks." August 3. Accessed July 16, 2013. http://www.news-leader.com/article/19980315.

Stebbins, Robert A. 2001. Exploratory Research in the Social Sciences. Qualitative Research Methods Series 48. Thousand Oaks, CA: Sage.

Substance Abuse and Mental Health Services Administration. 2009. Treatment Episode Data Set (TEDS) Highlights—2007 National Admissions to Substance Abuse Treatment Services. OAS Series #S-45, HHS Publication No. (SMA) 09–4360, Rockville, MD: Substance Abuse and Mental Health Services Administration.

———. 2011. Results from the 2010 National Survey on Drug Use and Health: Summary of National Findings. NSDUH Series H-41, HHS Publication No. (SMA) 11–4658. Rockville, MD: Substance Abuse and Mental Health Services Administration.

Taniguchi, Travis A., George F. Rengert, and Eric S. McCord. 2009. "Where Size Matters: Agglomeration Economies of Illegal Drug Markets in Philadelphia." Justice Quarterly 26:670–694.

Taylor, Bruce G., and Henry H. Brownstein. 2003. "Toward the Operationalization of Drug Market Stability: An Illustration Using Data from Crack Cocaine Markets in Four Urban Communities." Journal of Drug Issues 22:73–98.

Taylor, Bruce G., Henry H. Brownstein, Timothy M. Mulcahy, Johannes Fernandes-Huessy, Daniel J. Woods, and Carol Hafford. 2011a. "The Characteristics of

Methamphetamine Markets and Their Impact on Communities." Criminal Justice Review 36:312–331.

Taylor, Bruce G., Henry H. Brownstein, Timothy M. Mulcahy, Daniel J. Woods, Johannes Fernandes-Huessy, and Carol Hafford. 2011b. "Illicit Retail Methamphetamine Markets and Related Local Problems: A Police Perspective." Journal of Drug Issues 41:327–358.

Thoumi, Francisco E. 2005. "The Numbers Game: Let's All Guess the Size of the Illegal Drug Industry!" Journal of Drug Issues 35:185–200.

Tryon, Robert C. 1939. Cluster Analysis. New York: McGraw-Hill.

Tucson Citizen. 2012. "240-Yard Border Tunnel Near Yuma Tied to Meth Smuggling." July 19. Available on the Arizona Meth Project website, http://methproject.org/action/arizona/details/news-story-2012-07-19.html.

Tyner, Elizabeth A., and William J. Fremouw. 2008. "The Relation of Methamphetamine Use and Violence: A Critical Review." Aggression and Violent Behavior 13:285–297.

Varner, Kurt J., Brian A. Ogden, Joseph Delcarpio, and Suzanne Meleg-Smith. 2002. "Cardiovascular Responses Elicited by the 'Binge' Administration of Methamphetamine." Journal of Pharmacology and Experimental Therapeutics 301:152–159.

Venkatesh, Sudhir A. 2008. Gang Leader for a Day: A Rogue Sociologist Takes to the Streets. New York: Penguin Press.

VisitYuma.com. 2013. "Yuma at a Glance." Accessed June 30, 2013. http://www.visityuma.com/who_we_are.html.

Vogt, William Paul, and R. Burke Johnson. 2011. Dictionary of Statistics and Methodology: A Nontechnical Guide for the Social Sciences. 4th ed. Thousand Oaks, CA: Sage.

Weber, Max. 1947. The Theory of Social and Economic Organization. Edited and translated by A. M. Henderson and Talcott Parsons. New York: Free Press.

Weisburd, David, and Lorraine Green Mazerolle. 2000. "Crime and Disorder in Drug Hot Spots: Implications for Theory and Practice in Policing." Police Quarterly 3:331–349.

Weisheit, Ralph. 2008. "Making Methamphetamine." Southern Rural Sociology 23:78–107.

Weisheit, Ralph, and Edward Wells. 2010. "Methamphetamine Laboratories: The Geography of Drug Production." Western Criminology Review 11:9–26.

Weisheit, Ralph, and William L. White. 2009. Methamphetamine: Its History, Pharmacology, and Treatment. Center City, MN: Hazelden.

Weiss, Carol H. 1975. "Interviewing in Evaluation Research." In Handbook of Evaluation Research—Volume I, edited by Elmer Louis Struening and Marcia Guttentag. Beverly Hills, CA: Sage.

White, Harrison C. 1981. "Where Do Markets Come From?" American Journal of Sociology 87:517–547.

Williams, Terry Tempest. 1989. The Cocaine Kids—The Inside Story of a Teenage Drug Ring. Reading, MA: Addison-Wesley.

Zweben, Joan E., Judith B. Cohen, Darrell Christian, Gantt P. Galloway, Michelle Salinardi, David Parent, and Martin Iguchi. 2004. "Psychiatric Symptoms in Methamphetamine Users." American Journal on Addictions 13:181–90.

Index

acetone, 13, 40, 41
addiction to meth, 4; arrests and, 106;
    cravings and, 15; in families, 60–
    61, 90, 95; *vs.* recreational use, 72;
    smurfing and, 36–37
adulteration, 59, 71, 79–80, 85–86
age of users, 85, 91, 104
alcohol, 36, 94
ammonia, 30
ammonium nitrate, 34
Andrews, P.W.S., 11
anhydrous ammonia, 30, 32, 35, 55,
    65, 83, 99
anhydrous method. *See* Nazi method
Anti-Drug Abuse Act of 1988, 10
appearance of meth, 27, 48; color,
    38–39, 41, 81, 82, 109; *vs.* taste/
    quality, 85
apprenticeship in local production,
    55–56, 64–65
Arizona, 56–58, 59, 82, 109, 123;
    smurfing in, 89; superlabs in, 38, 40;
    wash lab in, 41
Arizona Republic (newspaper), 57
Arkansas, 36, 44, 50
Arrestee Drug Abuse Monitoring
    program, 122
arrestees, surveys of, 8, 22, 122–123
arrests, 7, 22, 32, 50, 106; of Colima
    Cartel, 19–20; families and, 96; in
    Galax, VA, 2–3; of meth cooks, 36,
    65, 99; recovery and, 93
Associated Press (AP), 19

Atlanta, GA, 13–15, 87; meth distribu-
    tion in, 4, 52–53, 70, 85, 123
azcentral.com, 57

baking soda, 85
bars, 48, 70–71; biker bars, 71, 75, 76
batteries, 30, 34, 55
Beith, Malcolm, 19
biker cooks, dl-meth and, 81
biker gangs, 29–30, 58, 76
Birch method. *See* Nazi method
black community, smurfing and, 89,
    103
black market for pseudoephedrine,
    102
Blue Ridge Mountains, 1, 123
border with Mexico. *See* Mexican
    border
Bourgois, Philippe, 7
box labs, 36
Bronx, the, 7
Brownstein, Henry, 7–8, 20
Buffalo County, NE, 45
business model *vs.* social clubs, 48–49
"Business Plan Remakes Meth Mar-
    ket" (Scheck), 38
business relationships in import meth
    markets, 53–54

California, 46, 106, 107; crystal meth
    production in, 57–58, 82; meth
    production in, 27, 38, 39, 40, 123;
    as point in wholesale distribution,

California (continued)
42, 45, 60; seizures of meth near, 23; smurfing in, 88; spread of meth from, 31–32; superlabs in, 39, 40, 58, 82, 89
Campion, Emily, 30–31
Carbondale, IL, 91, 124
Carroll County, Virginia, 1
cars: in local drug exchange, 86–87; recruitment for drivers of, 59–60; retrofitted, 42–43, 60; as site of meth production, 55, 84, 92; *vs.* trucks, 60; for wholesale distribution, 42–43
cartels. *See* Mexican cartels
"Cartels Flood US with Cheap Meth" (Salter), 19
cashless economy, 37. *See also* smurfing
Caulkins, Jonathan, 8, 21
cell phones, 86, 107–108, 115; seizures of, 87
census. *See* 2010 Census
central nervous system, 16
changes in meth production, 35–36, 83–84
chemistry, 34–35, 81
Chicago, IL, 31, 45; gay meth community in, 73; heroin study in, 7; as hub in meth route, 4, 85
child custody rights, 15, 93–94, 96
child neglect, 17, 27–28, 91–93. *See also* domestic violence
children, 90–94; as catalyst for recovery, 53, 96; custody rights for, 15, 93–94, 96; as meth users, 95–96; neglect of, 17, 27–28, 91–93; recruitment of, 61, 90. *See also* family; personal relationships
cluster analytic technique, 116–117
cocaine (powder), 7, 69; *vs.* meth, 2, 66; Mexican involvement with, 19, 109; price of, 80, 100; transportation

of, 14, 19, 45; undercover investigation of, 67–68, 103. *See also* crack cocaine
cold buying, 59; street sales, 69, 74
cold method, 35, 36
cold tablets, 3, 18, 29, 55, 78, 88
Coleman fuel, 34
Colima Cartel, 19–20
Colombia, 20
color of meth, 38–39, 41, 81, 82, 109
Columbia River, 78
Combat Methamphetamine Epidemic Act (2005), 18. *See also* pseudoephedrine legislation
commercial value of meth, 22–24. *See also* price of meth
common colds, 16
communication, 77, 86–90
communications technology, 87; cell phones, 86, 107–108, 115
communities: of drug users, 65, 68, 72, 78; as focus of study, x, 25–27, 112, 120–122; local bars in, 71, 75; local cooks and, 3, 65; local dealers in, 45; local labs in, 18, 29; local "lingo" in, 87; local markets in, 6, 24, 25, 27, 107, 109–110, 117; local police in, 114; public health/safety in, 15, 28, 78, 120; social lives in, 5, 6, 80, 113; unemployment and, 1; urban, 20, 37, 68, 71–74. *See also* rural communities
community events, 27, 113, 125
competition: between meth distributors, 5, 51, 92, 116; between mom-and-pop and import markets, 24
Congress, 18
consignment, 4, 67
consumer demand. *See* demand for meth
consumer markets, 42
consumers: local dealers and, 5, 45, 47–49, 58, 59, 76; local labs and, 18,

33; as part of market, 11, 97, 121; pseudoephedrine legislation and, 79, 81–82

contacts, 60, 70, 71, 100

conversion labs, 41

cooking process. *See* local meth production

cooks. *See* local cooks

crack cocaine, 17, 69, 74; dealers of, 42, 46, 79; price of, 80; study on, 7, 20; weights of, 80–81. *See also* cocaine (powder)

crack cocaine markets, 79, 115; *vs.* meth markets, 20, 47, 66; street sales in, 69, 74; violence in, 92

Craigslist, 72

"crank," 38–39, 85, 95

crime scenes, 37, 120

criminal justice, 22

criminology, 7, 9, 29

Crystal King (El Rey de Cristal), 20

crystal meth: local meth production and, 40–41; Mexican cartels and, 13, 79, 82, 109; *vs.* powder/paste meth, 38–39, 48–49, 79–80, 85, 100; produced in California, 57–58, 82; quality of, 39, 84, 100, 104. *See also* import meth markets

cultural objects, 80

culture, x, 77–96; communication as, 86–90; definition of, 80; family life as, 90–96; importance of, 76; language of, 80–81, 87–88; social experience and, 11

"cutting" meth, 59, 71, 79–80, 85

dangers of meth production, 27, 29, 32, 55, 83; children and, 91–92

Dauter, Luke, 11

dealers. *See* meth dealers

deaths from meth, 81

decline in local laboratories, 38, 40, 78, 99

demand for meth, 110; in East, 68, 122; import meth market and, 14, 16; local labs and, 31; pseudoephedrine legislation and, 38, 106; *vs.* supply, 78; in wholesale dollars, 23

Denver, CO, 44

Department of Defence Appropriations Act, 10

Department of Human Services (DHS), 94

Department of Justice, 10

deportation, 50, 100–101

depression, 15

Desroches, Frederick, 8

detectives. *See* narcotics detectives

Detroit, MI, 85

distribution of meth. *See* meth distribution

dl-meth, 81, 86

d-meth, 81, 86

dogs, 42

Dollar General Store, 35–36

domestic violence, 17, 27–28, 91–93. *See also* child neglect

Donnelly, John, 38

dopamine, 16

drivers: recruitment of, 59–60; for wholesale distribution, 42–44. *See also* meth distribution

Drug Abuse and Regulation Control Act (1970), 17

drug arrests. *See* arrests

drug cartels. *See* Mexican cartels

drug control, 10

Drug Enforcement Administration (DEA), 19, 22, 26, 30, 38, 40, 118, 120; meth seizures by, 23; Paillet and, 32

Drug Enforcement Agency, 10

drug enforcement officials. *See* respondents

drug markets. *See* illicit drug markets

drug policy, 6, 10

drug trafficking, 8, 15, 22, 73
drug trafficking organizations (DTOs), 39, 73, 82
drug treatment, 21, 22
drug treatment counselors. *See* respondents
Durkheim, Emile, 33

East (region), 122–123; distribution of meth in, 13; low demand for meth in, 68, 122
East Coast, 4, 44, 60, 67, 123
Eck, John, 7
economic sociology, 11
economic studies, 9
economy: of illicit drug markets, 7, 8, 24; of meth markets, 23–24
effects of meth: on the brain, 16; on environment, 18, 78; on health and safety, 15, 78; on social experience, 17
"eight ball," 23, 50, 64, 80–81, 96
El Paso, TX, 91
El Paso Intelligence Center (EPIC), 22, 23
El Rey de Cristal (Crystal King), 20
La Eme, 58
ephedrine, 30, 81
ephedrine/pseudoephedrine reduction method, 30, 41
ethnographic studies, 9
Eugene, OR, 123
euphoria, 16
Evansville, IN, 124
Executive Office of the President, 10
explosions, 36, 55, 91, 103, 104

family, 90–96; impact of meth use on, 15, 124; involvement in meth distribution, 60; in local labs, 48, 56, 64; recovery and, 53; as recruitment, 60–61, 90–91, 95; violence and, 17,
27–28, 91, 92–93. *See also* children; personal relationships
family service providers. *See* respondents
federal and state legislation. *See* pseudoephedrine legislation
Federal Bureau of Investigation (FBI), 22
Fligstein, Neil, 11
Food Lion, 4
Fort Wayne, IN, 85
freezer packs, 35–36
Fresno, CA, 38
friends: as contacts, 71, 95; as customers, 52, 63; in local labs, 48; as recruiters, 60–61, 63. *See also* personal relationships
Fries, Arthur, 23
Funk, Brian, 1
future of meth industry, 105–110

Galax, VA, 1–5, 94, 123
gangs: biker gangs, 29–30, 58, 76; La Eme, 58; illicit drug markets and, 7–8; Mexican gangs, 84; street gangs, 58
Garden City, KS, 45
gay subculture, 71–73
Georgia, 13; children in, 90, 93; conversion labs in, 41; local labs in, 14, 48; meth distribution in, 14, 43, 60, 70; meth production in, 34–36; respondents from, 37, 44, 49, 55–56, 85, 103; urban meth use in, 72; white dealers in, 52–53, 64, 69–70. *See also* Atlanta, GA
Ginsberg, Allen, 17
Goldstein, Paul, 7
Google maps, 26, 44, 64, 69, 118, 120
Grand Island, NE, 45
Grayson County, Virginia, 1
Great Appalachian Valley, 1

Harlem, NYC, 7
Hastings, NE, 45
Hawaii, 80
hazardous waste, 37, 78
health and safety problems, 78. *See also*
    public health and safety
Henderson, KY, 124
heroin, 7, 17, 45, 109; *vs.* meth, 2, 66–
    68; street sales of, 69, 74
Hertz, Denise, 18
hierarchy: in import meth market, 47,
    100; in local meth market, 45–46; in
    status of local cooks, 104–105
highways. *See* interstate highways
Hispanic men: child custody rights for,
    94; sexual relationships and, 62
Hispanics: in Galax, VA, 2; in Hold-
    rege, NE, 75–76; in meth distri-
    bution, 45, 47, 52, 60, 63, 100;
    personal relationships between, 70;
    in Yuma, AZ, 56
history of meth, 16–18
Holdrege, NE, 75–76
homeless shelter, 89; language at, 87
homes: as site of meth production,
    91–92, 93; as site of meth sales, 2,
    20, 100, 115
homicide, 8
homosexual community, 71–73
honchos, 46, 50
Honolulu, HI, 122
Hughes, Patrick, 7
human immunodeficiency virus
    (HIV), 72, 73
Hunt, Dana, 20

ice. *See* crystal meth
ice packs, 35–36
icing labs, 41
Idaho, families of meth users in, 90–91
illicit drug markets, 5–9; economy
    of, 7, 8, 24; *vs.* meth markets, 45; as

social organizations, 9–12, 20, 110;
    weights in, 80–81. *See also* crack
    cocaine markets
illicit drugs. *See* cocaine (powder);
    crack cocaine; heroin; marijuana
Illinois, 31–32, 41, 45, 83, 101; gay
    meth users in, 73; introduction of
    meth to, 66; young meth users in,
    91. *See also* Chicago, IL
immigrants from Mexico, 2, 49, 60,
    89–90
import meth markets, 98–101, 116–
    117; in Atlanta, GA, 13; business
    relationships in, 53–54; demand
    for meth and, 14, 16; in Galax,
    VA, 2; hierarchy in, 47, 100; *vs.*
    local production, 24, 25, 27, 33–
    34, 37–38, 40–41, 48–49, 78, 121;
    Mexican border and, 123; Mexican
    cartels and, 28, 45, 66, 99–100, 104;
    in Midwest, 31; in Oregon, 123;
    personal relationships in, 49–50,
    70–71; profit in, 19–20, 37–38, 41,
    49; pseudoephedrine laws and, 19,
    38–40, 81–82, 97–98, 106–109;
    purity of meth in, 84, 85–86; qual-
    ity of meth in, 79–80, 82–83, 85,
    109; on reservations, 73; rise in, 3,
    39–40; as social activity, 38, 53–54.
    See also local meth markets; meth
    markets
Inc. (online magazine), 13
Indiana, 30–31, 106; families in, 91,
    92; local labs in, 48; purity of meth
    in, 85; smurfing in, 89; spread of
    Nazi method to, 32
Indianapolis, IN, 85
industry, definition of, 11. *See also*
    meth industry
ingredients. *See* precursor drugs
Initiative for Research on Retail Drug
    Markets, 111

in-person interviews, 26–27
interagency drug crime law enforce-
    ment teams. *See* respondents
interstate highways, 13, 14, 44–45, 75,
    78, 94, 98, 119. *See also* transporta-
    tion routes
intravenous use, 91
iPods, 87

Jackson, Andrew, 32
Jacksonville, IL, 31–32, 83, 124
Japan, 16
jar-jumpers, 61
jconline.com, 30
Journal and Courier (newspaper), 30

Kansas, 75
Kansas City, 32, 44
Kentucky, 32, 83, 88; family life in,
    91, 92
Kotkin, Joel, 13

laboratories. *See* local laboratories
Langton, Jerry, 19–20
language of meth culture, 80–81,
    87–88
Las Vegas, NV, 122, 123
law enforcement officers. *See* respon-
    dents
laws. *See* pseudoephedrine legislation
legislation. *See* pseudoephedrine
    legislation
Lexington, KY, 44–45
Lincoln, Abraham, 6, 32
"lingo," 87
liquid smoke, 34
lithium, 30, 32, 34, 55, 83
Little Rock, AR, 50
l-meth, 86
local consumers. *See* consumers
local cooks, 3, 27, 33, 88; arrests of,
    36, 65, 99; crystal meth from, 79, 82;
    family and, 91–93; in Georgia, 14,

36; in mentorships, 55–56, 64–66;
    as part of social collectivities, 37,
    47–48; personal relationships with,
    48, 56, 61–62, 64–66; production
    methods and, 29, 35–36, 81, 83,
    84; pseudoephedrine laws and, 18,
    38–40, 78, 81–82, 101–102; purity
    of meth and, 84, 86; in rural areas,
    18; social status of, 104–105. *See also*
    local laboratories; local meth mar-
    kets; local meth production; meth
    production methods; smurfing
local laboratories, 3; box labs, 36; as
    cashless economies, 37; children
    and, 91; decline in, 38, 40, 78, 99;
    distribution and, 47; d-meth in,
    81; explosions in, 36; in Galax, VA,
    2; in Georgia, 14; *vs.* import meth
    markets, 24, 25, 27, 33–34, 37–38,
    40–41, 48–49, 78, 121; increase in,
    31–33, 40; mentorship in, 55–56,
    64–65; in Midwest, 31–32, 34–35,
    37, 101, 124; in Missouri, 88; near
    Atlanta, GA, 123; as networks, 48,
    56; in Oregon, 78, 123; produc-
    tion methods in, 29, 30, 35–36, 81,
    83, 84; pseudoephedrine legisla-
    tion and, 18, 34–35, 38, 40, 98,
    99, 101–103, 106–109; purity of
    meth in, 85–86; quality of meth in,
    48–49, 85; in rural areas, 13, 17–18,
    102–103, 124; seizures of, 26, 30,
    64, 118–119; as small businesses, 37,
    89; as social activity, 48, 64–66; as
    social collectivities, 37, 47–49; in
    South Carolina, 48. *See also* local
    cooks; local meth markets; local
    meth production; meth production
    methods; Nazi method; one-pot
    technique; shake-and-bake tech-
    nique; smurfing
local meth markets, 101–105, 115,
    116–117; in communities, 6, 24,

25, 27, 107, 109–110; hierarchy in, 45–46; *vs.* meth industry, 6, 10–11, 23–24, 26, 28, 117; *vs.* national meth industry, 10–11, 23–24, 26; new markets, 66–68; organization of, 5–6, 11; *vs.* other illicit drug markets, 45; participation in, 6, 11; as part of industry, 117; personal relationships in, 51–52, 61–62, 69–71, 75–76; recruitment of dealers in, 60–61; relationships between, 6, 9, 11, 25; social dynamics of, 84; as social organizations, 6, 9, 33, 44, 52, 107, 110; stability of, 8; wholesale distribution and, 45. *See also* import meth markets; local meth production; meth markets

local meth production: apprenticeship in, 55–56, 64–65; in Arkansas, 36; of crystal meth, 40–41; in Georgia, 34; *vs.* import meth markets, 24, 25, 27, 33–34, 37–38, 40–41, 47, 78, 121; as social activity, 34–37; *vs.* street corner drug markets, 37; taste/quality of meth in, 85. *See also* local cooks; meth production; meth production methods

local retail dealers. *See* meth dealers
local retail markets. *See* local meth markets
Los Angeles, CA, 42, 79
Los Angeles Free Press, the (newspaper), 17
lye, 34

Manhattan, NYC, 7
manufacture of meth. *See* meth production
marijuana, 53, 67–68, 74, 82, 94; Mexican involvement with, 109; transportation of, 14, 45
Marine Corps Air Station Yuma, 57
market, definition of, 11

market participants, 121; communication between, 86–87; familial relationships between, 90–96; social relationships between, 6, 10, 11, 52, 58–59, 61–62. *See also* meth dealers; meth markets; participants in meth markets

markets. *See* import meth markets; local meth markets; meth markets
Maryland, 123–124
Mazerolle, Lorraine, 7
McBride, Duane, 18
McKetin, Rebecca, 8–9
measures of meth, 80–81
Medford, OR, 106, 123
mentorship in local production, 55–56, 64–65
men who have sex with men (MSM), 71–73
methamphetamine: as artifact, 80; *vs.* heroin and cocaine, 2, 66–68; history of, 16–18; as product, 77–86; studies on, 8–9; weights of, 80–81
Methamphetamine Interagency Task Force, 17
meth business. *See* meth industry
meth cooks. *See* local cooks
meth dealers: adulteration of product by, 59, 71, 79–80, 85–86; children and, 90, 93–94; consumers and, 5, 45, 47–49, 58, 59, 76; ethnicity of, 2, 3–4, 45, 50–53, 64, 69–70, 75–76; in import meth market, 50, 62; at local labs, 37; local retail dealers, 27, 63; personal relationships with, 69–71; recruitment for, 45–46, 49–50, 51, 60–61
meth distribution, 6, 27; in Atlanta, GA, 4, 13, 14, 52–53, 70, 85, 123; competition in, 5, 51, 92, 116; conversion labs and, 41; drivers for, 42–44, 59–60; ethnicity and, 45, 47, 52, 60, 63, 70, 100; in Galax, VA, 4–5; homes

meth distribution (continued)
as site of, 2, 20, 100, 115; in Oregon, 78; personal relationships and, 51, 61–64; pseudoephedrine legislation and, 19, 38; as social activity, 33, 41–52; superlabs and, 39; in Tacoma, WA, 100; TCOs and, 19; transportation for, 41–45, 59–60, 86–87; trust and, 5, 20, 45, 51, 59, 62, 70, 71; via truck, 60; wholesale *vs.* retail, 9, 34–35, 37, 46, 48

meth industry: as commercial enterprise, 44; communication in, 86–90; definition of, 97; future of, 105–110; *vs.* legal industries, 38; *vs.* local retail markets, 10–11, 23–24, 26, 117; objective of, 33, 44; pseudoephedrine legislation and, 28, 97–98, 105–110; as social organization, 9, 44, 52, 107, 110

"Meth Labs Make Return to U.S." (Scheck), 38

meth manufacture. *See* meth production

meth markets: commonalities and variability between, 97–98, 115–116; consumers in, 11, 97, 121; *vs.* crack cocaine markets, 20, 47, 66; economy of, 23–24; evolution of, 12; as focus of study, 112, 114–115, 122; public health and safety and, 27, 110; social experience and, 11, 26; violence in, 116. *See also* import meth markets; local meth markets

methodology, 24–27, 80, 98, 111–123

meth production: in California, 27, 38, 39, 40, 123; in cars, 55, 84, 92; changes in, 35–36; dangers of, 27, 29, 32, 55, 83, 91–92; *vs.* demand for meth, 14; in Galax, VA, 2; in Georgia, 34–36; in homes, 91–93; in Indiana, 30–31; in Jacksonville, IL, 32; in Missouri, 31, 32, 35, 37; in rural communities, 29–30; as social activity, 33–41

meth production methods, 29, 35–36, 81, 83, 84; in superlabs, 30. *See also* Nazi method; one-pot technique; phenyl-2-propanone method (P2P); red phosphorous (Red-P) method; shake-and-bake technique

methylamine, 30

methylsulfonylmethane (MSM), 85

Mexican border, 23, 27, 84, 113, 123; at I-5, 78; at San Luis, 56–57; transportation across, 22, 42–43, 125

Mexican cartels, 31, 58, 101; Colima Cartel, 19–20; crystal meth and, 13, 79, 82, 109; Hispanic population and, 70, 75; in import meth market, 28, 45, 66, 99–100, 104; Sinaloa Cartel, 19–20; smurfing and, 89–90; superlabs run by, 30. *See also* Mexican nationals

Mexican drug trafficking organizations (DTOs), 39, 73

Mexican gangs, 84

Mexican immigration, 2, 49, 60, 89–90

Mexican nationals, 41, 51; as distributors, 4–5, 46; in superlabs in California, 58, 82. *See also* Mexican cartels

Middle Atlantic, 26, 35, 43, 67, 103, 123–124

Midwest, 18, 26, 122–123; local labs in, 31–32, 34–35, 37, 101, 124; pseudoephedrine laws in, 105–106

military base, 70

Minnesota, 64

Mississippi, pseudoephedrine laws in, 105–106

Missouri, 85, 101; meth production in, 31, 32, 35, 37; Paillet in, 83; smurfing in, 88–89

mixed methods studies, 111–112

mom-and-pop laboratories. *See* local laboratories
multi-method studies, 111–112

narcotics detectives (respondents), ix, 121–122. *See also* respondents
National Academy of Sciences (NAS), 6
National Clandestine Laboratory Register (NCLR), 118, 120
National Climatic Data Center, 56
National Control Strategy, 10
National Directory of Law Enforcement Administrators database, 114
National Drug Intelligence Center (NDIC), 10, 19, 23
National Drug Threat Assessment, 18, 19
national industry. *See* meth industry
National Institute of Justice (NIJ), ix, 17, 111, 122
National Institute on Drug Abuse (NIDA), ix, 16, 24, 111
national meth industry. *See* meth industry
National Oceanic and Atmospheric Association, 56
National Public Safety Information Bureau, 114
National Research Council, 6
National Survey of Drug Use and Health, 21–22
Native Americans, 73–74
natural resources, 78
"'Nazi Dope': Meth Reinvented in the Ozarks" *(Springfield News-Leader)*, 31
Nazi method, 30; age and, 104; crystal meth from, 40–41; in Ohio, 35; *vs.* other techniques, 32, 35; quality of meth from, 83; social status and, 105; spread of, 31, 32; in St. Louis, MO, 102; in Tennessee, 35

Nebraska, 44–45, 71, 75–76
neglect, 17, 27–28, 91–93
neighbors' response to meth production, 40, 84
networking in local labs, 48, 56
Nevada, 72, 123
Newark, NJ, 7
new markets, 66–68
New Mexico, 69, 70, 87, 92
New York, 7–8
Norfolk and Western Railway, 1
normative patterns of behavior, 33, 52–54, 80
norms, 33, 110
North Carolina, 1, 13, 44, 103, 123

Office of National Drug Control Policy (ONDCP), 8, 10, 20, 23, 122–123
Ohio, 35, 61, 65, 107
one-pot technique, 105; explanation of, 29–31; explosions from, 36; ingredients for, 104; rise in, 32, 83; as social organization, 37; in St. Louis, MO, 102–103. *See also* meth production methods; shake-and-bake technique
open air drug market, 20. *See also* street corner drug markets; street sales
Oregon, 81, 87, 98; child custody issues in, 93–94; crystal meth in, 85; families of meth users in, 90–91; Portland, 42, 69, 78–80, 91, 98, 122–123; pseudoephedrine laws in, 40, 78, 105–106, 123; respondents from, 39, 42, 46, 60, 65, 69, 71
Organized Crime Drug Enforcement Task Force, 114

P2P. *See* phenyl-2-propanone (P2P)
Pacific Northwest, 26, 60, 123
Paillet, Bob, 31–33, 83

paranoia, 14, 15, 17, 52, 92
Parsons, Talcott, 9
participants in meth market. *See* market participants
patterns of behavior, normative, 33, 52–54, 80
"peanut butter," 38–39, 49, 82
personal relationships, 6; between buyers and sellers, 47, 58–59, 100, 115; as entry into meth distribution, 63–64; with family, 90–96; in import meth markets, 49–50, 70–71; in local labs, 48, 55–56, 61–62, 64–66; in local meth markets, 51–52, 69–71, 75–76; in rural communities, 71; between white buyers and sellers, 51, 69–70. *See also* children; family; friends; sexual relationships; social relationships
pharmaceutical industry, 106. *See also* pseudoephedrine legislation
pharmacies, 18, 88, 89
phenyl-2-propanone method (P2P), 29–30; *vs.* crystal meth, 82; in Midwest, 32; *vs.* Nazi method, 35; in Ohio, 35; in Oregon, 81; Paillet and, 83; quality of, 104. *See also* meth production methods
phenylpropolamine, 18
Philadelphia, PA, 8
Phoenix, AZ, 56, 122, 123; smurfing in, 89
police respondents. *See* respondents
police survey. *See* survey of police agencies
population: of Atlanta, GA, 13; of Holdrege, NE, 75; of Jacksonville, IL, 31–32; of Portland, OR, 78; of St. Louis, MO, 101; of Tacoma, WA, 98; of Yuma, AZ, 56
portable labs, 30
Portland, OR, 69, 78–80, 91, 98, 122–123; meth distribution in, 42

powder meth: *vs.* crystal meth, 38–39, 48–49, 79–80, 85, 100; purity of, 39, 84, 100. *See also* local laboratories
precursor drugs, 18, 29–30, 55, 84; as cashless economy, 37; as part of smurfing, 88, 99; in retail stores, 35–36. *See also* pseudoephedrine legislation; specific precursor drugs
Pretrial Services database, 8
price of illicit drugs, 8, 80, 100
price of meth, 50–51, 80–81, 96, 100; commercial value, 22–24; pseudoephedrine legislation and, 99
production of meth. *See* meth production
profit: in import meth markets, 19–20, 37–38, 41, 49; in local production of crystal meth, 82. *See also* price of meth
prostitution, 61–62
pseudoephedrine, 88; as currency, 89, 102, 103; in d-meth, 81; local labs and, 48; in Nazi method, 32; in one-pot technique, 29; as precursor, 3, 55, 99; in Red-P method, 30. *See also* pseudoephedrine legislation
pseudoephedrine legislation, ix, 3, 14, 79; changes in meth industry and, 28, 97–98, 105–110; demand for meth and, 38, 106; import meth market and, 19, 39–40, 81–82, 97–98, 106–10; local production and, 18, 34–35, 38, 40, 98, 99, 101–103, 106–109; in Oregon, 40, 78, 105–106, 123; price of meth and, 99; quality of meth and, 82–83, 109; shift from powder to ice and, 81–82; superlabs and, 39, 107–109
public health and safety, ix, x, 25, 116; in communities, 15, 28, 78, 120; meth markets and, 27, 110; quality of meth and, 81

public safety and public health officials. *See* respondents

Puget Sound (WA), 98

purity of meth, 9, 79; in crystal meth *vs.* powder or paste, 39, 84, 100; in d-meth *vs.* l-meth, 86; in local labs *vs.* import market, 85–86; pseudoephedrine legislation and, 19, 39. *See also* color of meth; quality of meth

purity tests, 40

qualitative research methods, 25, 111–112, 113, 118

quality of meth, 77–78, 79–80, 81–84, 115; changes in technique and, 83; crystal meth *vs.* powder meth, 85; education of producers and, 83–84; in local labs *vs.* superlabs, 48–49; in one-pot method, 104; pseudoephedrine laws and, 82–83, 109; in shake-and-bake technique, 83–85; skill of cook and, 65; in superlabs, 38–39, 48–49; in Yuma, AZ, 57. *See also* purity of meth

quantitative research methods, 25, 111–112, 113

racial demographics: in Holdrege, NE, 75; in Jacksonville, IL, 32; in Portland, OR, 78; in Staunton, VA, 95; in St. Louis, MO, 101; in Tacoma, WA, 98

Radcliffe-Brown, A.R., 33

rates of meth use, 81, 122–123

recovery, 53, 93, 96

recreational meth use, 72

recruitment: of children, 61, 90; of drivers, 59–60; by family, 60–61, 90–91, 95; by friends, 60–61, 63; of local dealers, 45–46, 49–50, 51, 60–61; through sexual relationships, 62

red phosphorous (Red-P) method, 30, 32, 35, 83, 104, 105. *See also* meth production methods

refining process for crystal meth, 27

regional markets. *See* import meth markets; meth markets

Reno, NV, 72, 123

researcher in Georgia (respondent), 72

research methods, 25, 111–112

reservations, 73–74

respondents: drug enforcement official in Georgia, 14; drug enforcement official in Hawaii, 80; drug enforcement official in Virginia, 81; drug policy official in Oregon, 60; drug treatment counselors from Oregon, 65–66, 91, 93–94, 106; drug treatment counselors from Virginia, 44; family service providers in Oregon, 93–94; family service providers in Virginia, 62, 93; husband and wife in Georgia, 49, 52–53, 85; from Illinois, 45; interagency drug crime law enforcement team in Indiana, 91, 106; interagency drug crime law enforcement teams in Georgia, 41, 43, 60; law enforcement officers from Georgia, 14; law enforcement officers from Illinois, 31; law enforcement officers from Missouri, 31; meth cook from Georgia, 64, 103; meth dealer from Oregon, 42, 46–47, 71, 78–80, 85, 94; meth dealer from Virginia, 49, 51–52, 59, 60–61, 70, 108; meth user from Georgia, 15, 48; meth user from Virginia, 61; narcotics detective from Arizona, 41, 57, 109; narcotics detective from Arkansas, 36, 44; narcotics detective from California, 40, 88, 107–108; narcotics detective from Georgia, 35, 70, 90; narcotics detective from Illinois, 66; narcotics detective from Indiana, 89; narcotics detective from Kentucky, 88;

respondents (continued)
narcotics detective from Louisiana, 71; narcotics detective from Missouri, 37; narcotics detective from Nebraska, 71, 75–76; narcotics detective from Nevada, 72; narcotics detective from New Mexico, 69, 70, 87, 92–93; narcotics detective from Ohio, 35, 65, 107; narcotics detective from Oklahoma, 70; narcotics detective from Oregon, 40; narcotics detective from Tennessee, 35, 84, 93, 108; narcotics detective from Texas, 80; narcotics detective from Utah, 39, 46, 50, 93, 109; narcotics detective from Virginia, 3–4, 87; narcotics detective from Washington, 72, 81; police drug unit member in Georgia, 93; police investigator in Virginia, 85; police officers from VA, 62; police officers in Kentucky, 83, 91; police officers in Yuma, AZ, 59; police officials from Illinois, 41, 82–83; police officials in Washington, 45; police respondent from Arizona, 82; police respondent from Arkansas, 50; police respondent from Georgia, 41; police respondent from Illinois, 32; police respondent from Minnesota, 64; police respondent from Nebraska, 44; police respondent from Oregon, 39; police respondent from South Carolina, 36, 48; police respondent from Utah, 83–84; public safety and public health officials, 26; public safety and public health officials in Georgia, 14; sheriff in Missouri, 85; state trooper from Illinois, 73; state trooper from Indiana, 48, 85. *See also* narcotics detectives (respondents); police respondents

retail drug markets. *See* illicit drug markets
retail level. *See* local meth markets
retail meth distribution. *See* meth distribution
retrofitted cars, 42–43, 60
Reuter, Peter, 8
revenue. *See* profit
Rhodes, William, 21, 22
Riverside, CA, 82
rural communities: d-meth in, 81; local laboratories in, 13, 17–18, 102–103, 124; meth production in, 29–30; meth use in, 15, 68, 123; personal relationships in, 71; *vs.* urban communities, 37, 68, 72. *See also* communities

Sacramento, CA, rates of meth use in, 122–123
safety. *See* public health and safety
Salem, OR, 87, 123
Salter, Jim, 19
San Bernardino, CA, 57–58, 82
San Diego, CA, 7, 32, 122
San Francisco, CA, 40
San Luis, AZ, 56–57, 125
Scheck, Justin, 38
Schutz, Alfred, 80
Seattle, WA, 72, 87, 98, 123
seizure data, 120
seizures: of cell phones, 87; of illicit drugs, 21, 22; of meth labs, 26, 30, 64, 118–119; at Mexican border, 23; via wiretap, 107–108
sexual favors, 48, 61
sexually-transmitted diseases (STDs), 72
sexual relationships: in local retail markets, 61–62; between men who have sex with men, 71–73; between Mexican dealers and local white

women, 51–52. *See also* personal relationships

shake-and-bake technique, 29, 35, 36, 55; age of users and, 85, 104; pseudoephedrine laws and, 98; quality of meth and, 83–85. *See also* meth production methods; one-pot technique

Shenandoah National Park, 95

Shenandoah Valley, 44, 94

side effects of d-meth *vs.* dl-meth, 81

Sinaloa Cartel, 19–20

site visits, 112–113, 121–125

Skolnick, Jerome, 8

Skype, 87

"slamming," 91

small businesses: local labs as, 37, 89

smell of meth, 39, 84

smurfing, 55, 78, 87–90, 102; addiction to meth and, 36–37; definition of, 18; pseudoephedrine laws and, 98, 103, 106–109; as social organization, 37; in Tacoma, WA, 99. *See also* local laboratories; local meth production; pseudoephedrine legislation

social activity, 98; import meth market as, 38, 53–54; local labs as, 48; local meth markets as, 34–37; meth distribution as, 33, 41–47, 47–52; meth production as, 33–41

social behavior in import meth markets, 53–54

social clubs, 47–49

social collectivities, 37, 47–49

social experience, 17, 80, 111; markets and, 11, 26

social institutions, 33, 80

social interactions, x, 11, 74; in local labs, 64–66

social life, 33; in communities, 5, 6, 80, 113

social organization of meth sales, 52–54

social organizations, x; definition of, 9–10; illicit drug markets as, 9–12, 20, 110; local labs as, 37; meth markets and industry as, 6, 9, 33, 44, 52, 107, 110

social processes for wholesale distribution, 42

social relationships, 33, 54, 57; new markets and, 66–68; between participants in meth markets, 6, 10, 11, 52, 58–59, 61–62; recruitment of drivers and, 59–60. *See also* personal relationships

social science, 111, 113

social services, 96

social status, 53, 104–105

social structure of retail meth markets, 47

social transactions in meth market, 52

sociological analysis, x, 5, 109

sodium metal, 83

South Bend, IN, 85

South Carolina, 36, 43, 48

Southeast, 26, 34–35, 43, 123

Southwest, 26, 27, 45, 69, 123; local labs in, 34–35

Southwest Missouri State University, 31

Spanish Harlem, 7

Spokane, WA, 122

Springfield, MO, 31, 32

Springfield News-Leader (newspaper), 31

state troopers. *See* respondents

status of local cooks, 65

Staunton, VA, 4, 60–62, 94–96, 123

"stepping on" meth, 59, 71, 79–80, 85

St. Louis, MO, 31, 89, 101–105, 124

street corner drug markets, 69, 74, 116; *vs.* local meth production, 37

street gangs, 58

street sales, 69, 74; cold buying, 59
strip clubs, 48, 53
study, overview of, 24–27, 109–123
subcontracting, 44, 49–50
subculture, 71–74; bikers, 71; men
   who have sex with men, 71–73;
   Native Americans, 73–74
Substance Abuse and Mental Health
   Services Administration, 21–22
Sudafed, 88, 89, 108
superlabs, 19, 59–60, 79, 84, 100; in
   California, 40, 58, 82, 89; definition of, 39; *vs.* local laboratories,
   33–34; production methods in, 30;
   pseudoephedrine legislation and, 39,
   107–109; quality of meth in, 38–39,
   48–49; structure of, 37–38; wholesale distribution through, 41. *See also*
   crystal meth; import meth markets
survey of police agencies, ix, 25, 80,
   97–98, 112, 114–117, 121, 123–124
Sydney, Australia, 8–9
System to Retrieve Information from
   Drug Evidence (STRIDE), 22, 23

Tacoma, WA, 98–101
Taniguchi, Travis, 8
taste of meth, 39, 81, 85, 104
Taylor, Bruce, 8
TCOs. *See* transnational criminal organizations (TCOs)
technique, changes in, 36, 83–84
technology, 35–36, 83–84; cell phones,
   86, 87, 107–108, 115; communications technology, 87; wiretaps,
   107–108
telephone interviews (with respondents), ix, 25–26, 80, 83, 117–
   121, 123, 124; with detective in
   Nebraska, 75; with detective in
   Tennessee, 84; with detective in
   Walla Walla, 79; in Galax, VA, 2; with
   narcotics detective in New Mexico,

69; with narcotics police, 112; with
   police respondent in Minnesota, 64
Tennessee, 4, 32, 35, 84, 93, 108
territories, 8, 116
Texas, 4, 13, 14, 80, 91
text messaging, 86, 107–108. *See also*
   cell phones
Threat Assessment (NDIC), 18, 19, 23
"Top 25 Cities for Doing Business in
   America" (Kotkin), 13
trafficking of illicit drugs, 8, 15, 22;
   DTOs, 39, 73, 82
transnational criminal organizations
   (TCOs), 19
transportation for wholesale distribution, 41–45, 59–60. *See also* meth
   distribution
transportation routes: across Mexican
   border, 22, 42–43, 125; through
   Atlanta, GA, 4, 85, 123; through
   California, 42, 45, 60; through
   Chicago, IL, 4, 85; through Kentucky, 32; through Virginia, 44, 51.
   See also interstate highways; meth
   distribution
Treatment Episode Data Set, 22, 23
tribal police, 73
trucks: *vs.* cars, 60; recruitment for
   drivers of, 59–60; for wholesale
   distribution, 43–44
trust, 45, 71; between dealers and
   users, 5, 20, 51, 59, 70; between
   distributors and dealers, 51, 62. *See
   also* personal relationships
Tucson, AZ, 56
"240-Yard Border Tunnel near Yuma
   Tied to Meth Smuggling" *(Arizona
   Republic),* 57
two-liter bottles, 29, 55, 84
2010 Census: for Galax, VA, 1–2; for
   Holdrege, NE, 71; for Jacksonville,
   IL, 31–32; for Portland, OR, 78; for
   Tacoma, WA, 98; for Yuma, AZ, 56

undercover investigation, 67–68, 103
unemployment, 1, 2
Uniform Crime Reports, 22
U.S. Army Yuma Proving Ground, 57
U.S. Border Patrol, 27, 57, 113, 125
U.S. Department of Justice, 122
U.S. government, 107
U.S.-Mexican border. *See* Mexican border
urban communities: crack cocaine in, 20; drug sales in, 74; gay subculture in, 71–73; *vs.* rural communities, 37, 68, 72
urine samples, 22, 122
Utah, 46, 50, 83, 109; child neglect in, 93; import meth market in, 39–40

violence: domestic, 17, 27–28, 91–93; illicit drug markets and, 7–8; in meth markets, 116
Virginia, 13, 49, 51–52, 59, 70, 85; cell phone use in, 86–87, 108; color of meth in, 81; domestic violence in, 93; families in, 90; Galax, 1–5; as hub on meth route, 44, 51; Staunton, 4, 60–62, 94–96, 123. *See also* Galax, VA

Walgreens, 108
Walla Walla, WA, 79
Wall Street Journal, 38
Walmart, 35, 43, 88, 89, 103, 108
Washington (state), 39, 45, 72, 79, 81, 123; import meth market in, 98–101; tribal lands in, 73

Washington, DC, 8, 123–124
Washington Heights, NYC, 7
wash lab, 41
Waynesboro, VA, 4
web-based conferencing software program (WebEx), 26, 118, 119
Weber, Max, 33
weights of illicit drugs, 80–81
Weisburd, David, 7
Weisheit, Ralph, 18, 29
West (region), 18, 122, 123; P2P production in, 29–30; transportation by cars in, 42–43
West Coast, 31, 42, 60, 82
whites (Caucasians): as local dealers, 45, 50, 51, 64, 69–70, 75–76; as meth users, 45, 47, 49, 51, 69–70, 75–76, 100; personal relationships between, 51, 69–70; as truck drivers, 44
white women, 51–52, 62, 94
wholesale meth distribution. *See* meth distribution
wide-spread meth distribution. *See* meth distribution
Willamette River (OR), 78
Williams, Terry, 7
Wilson, Woodrow, 94–95
wiretapping, 107–108
World War II, meth production during, 16–17, 31

XBox, 87

Yuma, AZ, 56–58, 59, 123, 125

About the Authors

HENRY H. BROWNSTEIN is a senior fellow in the Substance Abuse, Mental Health, and Criminal Justice Studies Department at NORC at the University of Chicago. He was the principal investigator on the study of the Dynamics of Methamphetamine Markets funded by the National Institute on Drug Abuse (NIDA) on which this book is based. He is past chair of the Section on Sociological Practice and Public Sociology of the American Sociological Association, and past chair of the Section on Alcohol, Drugs and Tobacco. Brownstein has written a number of books and dozens of articles and book chapters on topics including drugs and violence, drug markets, crime statistics, qualitative research methods, and the relationship between research and policy. He earned his PhD in sociology from Temple University in 1977.

TIMOTHY M. MULCAHY is a principal research scientist in the Economics, Labor, and Population Studies department at NORC at the University of Chicago and was co-investigator of the methamphetamine market study. Prior to that, he completed two congressionally mandated studies for the National Institute of Justice, one examining the federal death penalty system and the other human trafficking. He has served as keynote speaker, panel chair, and panelist at numerous conferences, workshops, and seminars, and has published in journals such as *Criminal Justice, Criminal Justice Policy Review, Journal of Drug Issues, Journal of Technology Transfer*, and *Journal of Transactions on Data Privacy*, and *Contexts Magazine*. Mulcahy earned his MA in Policy Studies from the Johns Hopkins University Institute for Policy Studies, studied international economics and foreign policy studies at SAIS, and earned his BA in English from the University of Virginia.

JOHANNES HUESSY is a principal research analyst in the Economics, Population and Labor Studies department at NORC at the University of Chicago and was research associate for the methamphetamine market study. He was intimately involved with all of the processes of the study and made significant contributions to the study's innovative design and methodology. A presentation he gave on this work received a first-place blue ribbon award at the Association of Public Policy and Management for its innovative approach to improving public policy through web-enhanced, geocoded qualitative interviews. He earned his BA in Liberal Arts from St. John's College in Annapolis, MD, and his MA in Political Science from American University in Washington, DC.

AVAILABLE TITLES IN THE CRITICAL ISSUES IN CRIME AND SOCIETY SERIES

Laura S. Abrams and Ben Anderson-Nathe, *Compassionate Confinement:* A Year in the Life of Unit C

Tammy L. Anderson, ed., *Neither Villain Nor Victim: Empowerment and Agency among Women Substance Abusers*

Scott A. Bonn, *Mass Deception: Moral Panic and the U.S. War on Iraq*

Mary Bosworth and Jeanne Flavin, eds., *Race, Gender, and Punishment: From Colonialism to the War on Terror*

Loretta Capeheart and Dragan Milovanovic, *Social Justice: Theories, Issues, and Movements*

Walter S. DeKeseredy and Martin D. Schwartz, *Dangerous Exits: Escaping Abusive Relationships in Rural America*

Patricia E. Erickson and Steven K. Erickson, *Crime, Punishment, and Mental Illness: Law and the Behavioral Sciences in Conflict*

Jamie J. Fader, *Falling Back:* Incarceration and Transitions to Adulthood among Urban Youth

Luis A. Fernandez, *Policing Dissent: Social Control and the Anti-Globalization Movement*

Timothy R. Lauger, *Real Gangstas: Legitimacy, Reputation, and Violence in the Intergang Environment*

Michael J. Lynch, *Big Prisons, Big Dreams: Crime and the Failure of America's Penal System*

Raymond J. Michalowski and Ronald C. Kramer, eds., *State-Corporate Crime: Wrongdoing at the Intersection of Business and Government*

Susan L. Miller, *Victims as Offenders: The Paradox of Women's Violence in Relationships*

Torin Monahan, *Surveillance in the Time of Insecurity*

Torin Monahan and Rodolfo D. Torres, eds., *Schools under Surveillance: Cultures of Control in Public Education*

Leslie Paik, *Discretionary Justice: Looking Inside a Juvenile Drug Court*

Anthony M. Platt, *The Child Savers: The Invention of Delinquency*, 40th anniversary edition with an introduction and critical commentaries compiled by Miroslava Chávez-García

Susan F. Sharp, *Hidden Victims: The Effects of the Death Penalty on Families of the Accused*

Jeffrey Ian Ross, ed., *The Globalization of Supermax Prisons*

Dawn L. Rothe and Christopher W. Mullins, eds., *State Crime, Current Perspectives*

Robert H. Tillman and Michael L. Indergaard, *Pump and Dump: The Rancid Rules of the New Economy*

Mariana Valverde, *Law and Order: Images, Meanings, Myths*

Michael Welch, *Crimes of Power and States of Impunity: The U.S. Response to Terror*

Michael Welch, *Scapegoats of September 11th: Hate Crimes and State Crimes in the War on Terror*

Saundra D. Westervelt and Kimberly J. Cook, *Life after Death Row: Exonerees' Search for Community and Identity*

CPSIA information can be obtained at www.ICGtesting.com
Printed in the USA
BVOW07*0647120714

358087BV00001B/1/P